ME AND THE MANAGEMENT

An autobiographical look at life's serendipitous and synchronistic journey accompanied by a plethora of other-worldly helpers

Angela Baker

Autobiograpy
2018

Copyright © 2020 by Angela Baker

All rights reserved. This book or any portion thereof may not be reproduced or used in any manner whatsoever without the express written permission of the publisher.

ISBN: 978-1-913479-10-7 (paperback)
ISBN: 978-1-913479-11-4 (ebook)

My very close friend Peter John Bailey, when his brother Anthony Martin Bailey had finished the final proof-reading, said: "Anthony has just put the cherry on the cake". If so, then Peter put the icing on the cake. He edited, smoothed and ordered the contents beautifully designing the interior layout and the cover to flow harmoniously, exactly as I would wish. Anthony Martin Bailey was a wonderfully nitpicking editor, just the person I needed in my life. I, Angela Baker, with guidance from The Management baked this cake. I wrote it and painted Mortal Coil, the picture featured on its cover.

It's a book of life – how it turns up and what to learn from it – and always with love in an abundance.

Contents

Prologue i
Chapter One: Prearrangement 1
Chapter Two: Segway 9
Chapter Three: Basics 17
Chapter Four: Accepting the challenge 23
Chapter Five: The child I was 31
Chapter Six: Meeting The Management 37
Chapter Seven: Past lives 45
Chapter Eight: Those before me 49
Chapter Nine: Quantum view 57
Chapter Ten: We all count 65
Chapter Eleven: Relative balance 69
Chapter Twelve: Soulmate 75
Chapter Thirteen: Becoming me 81
Chapter Fourteen: Ancora Impro 87
Chapter Fifteen: Clearing the pattern 95
Chapter Sixteen: Baggage overboard 101
Chapter Seventeen: Leaving London 109
Chapter Eighteen: We are Giants 115
Chapter Nineteen: Starters orders 123
Chapter Twenty: Stoicism plus 129
Chapter Twenty-One: Living and dying 135

Chapter Twenty-Two: Taking up the mantle 139
Chapter Twenty-Three: Revelations 147
Chapter Twenty-Four: Flying again 153
Chapter Twenty-Five: We are our masters 159
Chapter Twenty-Six: The essence 165
Chapter Twenty-Seven: Track in the sand 175

Prologue

> Life can only be understood backwards
> but it must be lived forwards.
>
> SOREN KIERKEGAARD

IF I was writing a book to make a lot of money, it would probably have to be a good detective novel — with at least a few grim murders in it — but money is not the primary aim. Also, my guides had commented on my lack of imagination. The latter gift is very necessary for producing a good novel. So, this is the result and with the help of my writing guides. It's all been put on paper — as *The Management* had asked.

This book is a recollection my life that has been accompanied by my many spiritual guides and helpers. It has not always been easy and has usually been a challenge. The only way of tackling something as onerous as living is — however it starts — to keep on going, because sooner or later the page will turn over.

Thank goodness that, when at the start of life, we don't consciously look ahead — as to see the whole is far too daunting and the road ahead is many times too high, uncertain and narrow. What is written in this book is a retrospective look at the journey so far. It is the history of a life full of amazing changes and great love. Looking back helps to see the terrain as it really was, full of delightful turns and twists, from nerve-racking high drama to joy.

My guides have been with me all the way and this story can only be told according to my view so, being human, it will always be self-edited. The work is part mine and part channelled, although my guides tell me that it's all channelled — as that is what I do. I refer to my guides throughout with great affection as *The Management*.

I started writing this memoir shortly after *The Management* had smartly told me not to behave like a teenager any more; their request was for me to write a book with them. Given that my age had tipped over into the seventies at the time and my request to them had just been for a bit of male energy in my life, it seemed a rather odd statement. We do all have free will here and certainly do not have to comply, but being me and being a dyslexic, as usual, I rose to the challenge and jumped to it as they knew I would. The first thing that they asked was that I make an arrangement to meet up with my writing guides each morning at the same time. I realise that this was to instil a strict habit; well there was no stopping me once I started.

Thank goodness for computer spell-checker — a useful modern innovation. I can now check my *spells*. I must now apologise for the frequent use of — I — it is a bit of a habit as being the third child down in a large family, the elders have a tendency to speak for you; but, I was always very sure of what — I — wanted and did not need older sisters to speak for me. I — had to speak up for – *me*.

So this is it, my personal truth concerning my current life and in common with all other beings I have had many lives — and in many dimensions. When it will be proven that lives are concurrent or consecutive who knows? But, at this time, the quantum physicists are still debating this point.

Accompanying me in this life, as well as all my wonderful human friends, there are a delightful group of other dimensional friends; they are continuously with me on my journey — those delightful energies being what *The Management* jokingly refers to as my "plethora of other worldly helpers". My feelings for them are of deep love and gratitude; this is in return for their love, protection, and the wonderful sense of humour that they need when we work together in this earthly dimension.

Sad to say, it is necessary for me to take on board their continuous admonitions to stop being so serious and to have some fun — that's strange, as that is what I thought telling this story was.

So that's my homework, OK! I'll have some fun!

Chapter One

Real spirituality is the greatest rebellion there is.
It's risky; it's adventurous; it's dangerous.

Osho

To start a book discussing death can be looked upon as rather odd. Books are often started by a birth but what are the differences between birth and death? They are just transitions. Does the chrysalis die for the butterfly to live? No, it's just a process of transition. Why should we be any different from any other living thing? With each significant door closing in our life another — often surprisingly — promptly opens.

This door opened with a resounding crash. I have been told since, that I planned it and wanted it to be this way — and at this time — and firing on all fronts. So, I have nobody else to complain to except myself, even if it was all a bit full on. I was, as you will soon see, going through life in the usual way thinking nothing unusual was around the corner. Life just goes on, then — wham! — I was brought face to face with all my helper's guardians, logistical coordinators; in fact, all those that are usually hidden from us whilst we are on our latest sojourn in this dimension.

They are the guardian energies that are with us from our birth, I fondly call them *The Management*. I know that others often call them *Angels* — they don't have wings, it's just the elevated vibrational field around them that shows up when they visit us as on earth. Earth has a very low and dense vibration. Angels are just one of a numerous names that they have been given, we won't go into that here, just know that you are cared for and loved by them, and they are always with us. So, with any help or thing that we need we must remember to ask for it to be given — mostly!

My major guide and helpers are with me all day and night. I can constantly, physically feel them vibrating around me, touching me, always quick to answer when I have a question, ever ready with a nudge or a bit of information for me or those around me in this dimension, they are not too serious and always love a bit of fun: but, every so often they bring tears of amazement to my eyes, I must just accept and never question.

So here we are. It all started one day whilst in a place of deep despair and mourning, my husband of forty-nine years had recently passed away. I was in dark, grey place of reassessing my future and despondently thinking that the next time, when I was going to shop and driving along the bendy, twisting roads, with the deep drops and gullies that surround me here in the hills of southern France, that — Yes! it might be best not to go around the corner, but to just continue and drive straight on over the top.

The result of that passing thought made me realised how powerful my manifesting was getting, as a few days later on a sunny day I was driving to the shops, the car windows open a bit, the sun was shining and I was singing, then in flew a bee and distracted me, at the very moment I was driving around a bend. So, without breaking I drove off the road and into the only tree at the top of a big drop. The car hit the tree and was thrown back into the road and overturned, after hearing the fuel sloshing around — there was silence — just absolute silence.

On recovering consciousness, I slipped out of my undone seatbelt, and to this day I have no idea how I got out of the seat belt whilst hanging upside down, or how I passed through the small gap at the top of the window. I am quite substantial; remember this gap in the window was now upside-down at the bottom and level with the road. All that I can remember was the sight of my dead husband John's hands; these I instantly recognised, they were on the seat pockets of my jeans, pushing me out of the window in a rather undignified manner. I crawled across the road to lie in the ditch as I was fearful that the car would catch fire.

Two vertebrae were broken and the pain was extreme, as I was crawling I swore at the top of my voice calling John everything under the sun for letting this happen to me. He was then with me standing there so clearly on a bank, by the side of the road, laughing at me saying "You're not coming up here yet". This made me furious, as I had no belief of up here or down there, but of course it was up, he was on a higher vibrational level.

Some months later my guides told me that the occasion was a pivotal time in my life, a time of choice whether to stay or go through the gate. This time I visualised the portal as a small low mossy wooden gate — this dimension, as well as others, are full of portals. The Christians call them pearly gates. Why are they called pearly gates? In The Book of Revelation 21:21 there are twelve pearl gates, each one a single pearl. My guides said that there was not enough time for me to die and be reborn, the time was now for the work I had to do, and so they prevailed upon me to do it as I had originally wished to.

I accepted, taking up that new life as an adult with no time for a turnaround, I am now a different and extended version of me. In fact now a very different version of me, the odd thing is there is no fear of fatal car accidents or any other thing happening that might send me hurtling into the next dimension, though I would be happy to pass on whenever they and I might wish.

In the meantime I intend to do whatever they ask of me and whatever takes my fancy, I am as well as all others here a free agent.

I was strapped into a moulded plastic body brace, given a crutch, and was returning home after my stay in hospital. A neighbour, who was driving me home, thought that I must be mad, but humoured my request, to go up via the hills to the site of the accident on our way home. I was concerned because one of my green malachite earrings was lost at the time; it had fallen into the long grass where I had lain in the ditch. She stopped the car in a safe place and went and searched, but returned saying it was not to be found. I never take no for an answer, and so tottered up on my crutch and — hey presto — I pointed it out at once. This discovery left her silent for a long time. She then, later, made a remark as to what she thought I was!... No, not this time around.

After a few days at home as I was standing at the window in my back brace looking out at the garden and thought why have this large garden and be shut away alone behind electric gates. I promptly made a decision that over the next few months I would have someone to help me decorate the house with a view to selling it.

A little later that year, on a hot August afternoon, I was sitting at the computer researching the care and pruning of a walnut tree. Out of the blue — bang! — a punch in the chest that felt like a big fist, no warning signs, nothing, so falling to the floor and grabbing the phone I called a friend. He came, climbed over the front gate and called an ambulance, so off to hospital for the second time in a few months. My heart had just stopped, restarted, and then went out of rhythm for the next six months. When we have been under super stress and its over, within the following year a heart problem is very common. It's really like the elastic breaking, impossible to slow down; one can only just crash into a wall to stop it. It is very common to die within a year of a mate, sounds romantic: it's a broken heart — a real thing – it happens.

One must deliberately take steps to untangle ourselves from our partners and discover our own soul deep inside. So, take the time to re-access your life and discover who you are right now.

This was to be the start of some months of heart arrhythmia accompanied by complete exhaustion that was so bad I was unable to cross a road alone, my body was painfully slow in its movements. There were repeated attacks of arrhythmia, each time they appeared out of the blue, I was brought totally into myself and alone deciding what was next, to stay or go. I realised that it was a time of in-between — *here and there* — and the balance was more in favour of *there* for a while.

Living on my own, and behind locked gates, was very hard but the odd thing was, each time when laying on the floor with yet another arrhythmia attack the cat appeared from wherever he was way over in the garden. He lay next to my chest purring very loudly as if to make my heart go back into a regular pattern. Cats have an extraordinary healing energy although very independent of humans, they are very closely linked to us; over my desk is a photo of a cat lying on its back, arms stretched out, fast asleep, it is there to remind me to physically rest in the way that only cats can.

One day, at eight in the morning, whilst I lay on the floor with a particularly violent attack and with my heart beating all over the place I lost my temper and shouted at the top of my voice saying "If I have to have this bloody thing I MUST HAVE SOME MUSIC — NOW!" Immediately I heard Glen Gould's performance of Bach's Goldberg variations at full volume, it was filling the room with its wonderful energy. Wow! It was tremendous, the odd thing was that at that time I just accepted it as normal. Some days I stand back from myself with amazement at how everything is just accepted. Whatever comes along I never a question or doubt, never fearful, just joyful, and so grateful every time for all the love joy and care that they give me. Don't ask me who, or what they are, or what they are called, or prove who they are — they are *The Management* — to me.

This is written with great love, and gratitude for their constant sorting out and the protection that goes on in the background of my life, I am very much a human and often falter and usually it's about money, but they never let me down. A lesson to learn here and it is that we are supplied with abundance of whatever we need and at the right time. We need to remember that it's not for us to worry about how, that's not our job, and we must learn to just accept with gratitude and grace.

So, now my manifesting was changing as I was remembering how to bring up the power from the earth at will, feeling it rising through my feet highly controlled. Also, I am now aware that I must be very, very careful to only use this for good because having always had a rather fiery temper, that rises just as fast, this ability could do damage, so it must be used with great thought, it is not something to be played with or to go on an ego trip with. Thank goodness I arranged for it to stay in abeyance until I attained the wisdom of my later life, I think I have misused this skill before in another time.

Once I used this ability in anger, when sleeping in a room that had been inhabited by a long dead hangman who hadn't fully passed over, he was stuck and was unable to realise the time was for him to move on. He was very cross at my presence in his house and his room, so he was throwing my things around. I sat up in bed and, with such rage, really let rip at him soundlessly in my head about what he should do and where he should go. He shot off and didn't give me any more trouble for the rest of my sojourn in that house.

After six months and well on the road to recovery, life proceeded to take yet another bizarre turn, when working in the kitchen one day, bending down for a cookery book I suddenly lost the sight in my right eye and there was something pale blue flapping in my field of vision. Well, there I was alone with my sight going in one eye, so I called a friend to take me to a doctor, this time the macula had split probably as the result of a blow to the head from the car accident.

So, there was yet another visit to the hospital and it was slowly healed, thanks to the amazing French health service yet again; now the second eye looks to be going the same way. The two eyes see differently, one's vision has an upward curve and the other a downward curve, this makes motorway driving a bit stressful. The upkeep on this body is getting a bit pricey, but it has a long way to go yet, and it's always the same when keeping good old cars on the road.

Shortly after that time an odd dream came along, I awoke with the word Horus in my head and a very strong feeling of Egypt. So, why a dream of Horus? Then within days, coincidentally, I was given a stone that looked exactly like an Egyptian painted eye, well that started me off — the search was on now in earnest now, like a carrot to a donkey.

The Egyptian god Horus was depicted as part man, part hawk, he lost the sight of the right eye, the gods then promised to restore his sight if he promised to guard the land of Egypt in the future. So, there we go, my sight has been mended after a fashion, but I've yet to go to Egypt — who knows I might one day, I've always been attracted to that country, perhaps I was there at another time.

The day for selling the house came and it sold on the first day to the first person that came to see it. It's odd how often that happens in my life. A decision is made and then — wham — it's happened.

A lot of time had been spent exploring the area in recent months the right village and building were found, the latter a barn with a reasonable bit of garden set up from the road. It is at the edge of a small village up in the hills nearby to where I was then living. The barn had only one problem, it had a sold notice on it — OK! — try again. The friend, who had been searching with me, lived in that village and went by chance — or is it? — to one of the village aperitif occasions that very evening. An elderly lady asked her what she had been doing that day so she mentioned searching with me and finding the barn.

My serendipitous fortune came in with a resounding bang yet again, it appeared that the barn belonged to the elderly lady who now lived in another village and had just turned up for the evening's get together, she didn't know that the agent had neglected to remove the sign when her sale fell through a year before. Well, she was very interested and said that she would do a private sale. The following day when discussing my plans with a good friend in the housing business. She told me she had much experience of such things, and demanded that she negotiate the price for me and asked what price I wanted to start at. Well the first number in my head was sixty-five thousand, with a laugh she said "Some hopes", and promptly went to the seller, asked her what she wanted for the building the owner said sixty-five thousand, well that amazed my friend who was negotiating — but not me.

> *Always, just go with the first thought, as that thought is the one that's the right one, never doubt, let the logical brain take over, trust your instinct with both people and things; the gut feeling is your soul communicating with you, so ask when you want to know something and always, listen don't shut yourself off from help and make life hard. Your soul is old and wise, it's been there, done it, and knows all about it, and only wants to make life easier for you.*

I was working my way out of health problems that I found myself in when the next thing to arrive, out of the blue, was asthma in a big way. This stayed on with me for a couple of years — the result of lots of repressed tears. Asthma is now only a brief irritation during the grape harvest, the flowering of the yellow broom and with snow — snow changes the ions in the air that triggers asthma.

Chapter Two

*We must be willing to let go of the life we planned,
to have the life waiting for us*

Joseph Campbell

HERE we go packing up the home yet again — only one husband — but countless homes and I suppose that it has not stopped yet on the home front, there may well be more to come and probably more gardens.

In the time between the two homes it was necessary to find whatever temporary accommodation I could; the first to come was a converted stable — very suitable, having been born in the year of the horse.

Moving day was over, it was March and I was lying under the almond blossom on a lounger in the sunshine thinking that was an easy move for once. I then noticed a very black cloud that crawled across the sky and the snow started, never have I seen such a determined effort, we were snowed in for three days it was so deep it was nearly up to my knees, by some extraordinary chance in my summer packing were a pair of Wellington boots and winter vests, when only my spring and summer clothes for the south of France had been packed. I thought how did they get in there? — my helpers had come to the rescue yet again. Being so looked after constantly amazes and fills me with gratitude.

This was to be the start of a rather difficult period in my life. Thank goodness Dillion the dog and Max the cat settled down to the new circumstances and we were able to stay in the stable house until it was wanted for the owner's family summer holiday.

So summer came and we were on the move yet again, the animals went into kennels for the next five weeks this was so painful for us to part for so long. The move this time was to the lower ground floor of a house that belonged to an elderly lady who lived quietly, in privacy, upstairs. One day she started chatting over the balcony and mentioned the Sussex village that she had lived in before moving to France, well that was a flash of synchronicity — as life always is — it was the same village of my childhood home Oakdown. Every week she had visited a bed-bound friend who lived there, Oakdown was now a nursing home and it turned out that the friend lived there permanently.

Nothing in life ever turns out to be a surprise a constant layering, twisting and turning. The next move for me was to be temporary in an extraordinary little house, it had two rooms one above the other with outside stairs, it was set high on two terraces in the midst of an orchard, a place of great peace.

There was a downside that was odd when staying in the little house I was not allowed my animals with me, this was rather strange as the property was overrun by wild dogs at night and this meant shutting myself in on the upper level before nightfall. Because of this in total my stay was only for three weeks although it was a wonderful place, I was unhappy due to my being separated from the animals and being homeless at the same time, this is not a good thing for me.

I realise now that I was neglecting to ground and drifting like a badly tethered balloon — grounding is now an absolute necessity — the only thing I did was to instinctively lean with my back to a giant conifer each day and also kept some of its bark in my bag to hang on to when panicking.

It was at this time that the realisation came of what I was taking on with the barn and the rebuilding with its inevitable spiralling cost, as usual I was hurtling forward stifling my fear and beating myself, my tendency is to drive myself with no kindliness a Turkish donkey would have fared better.

Standing here on safe ground looking back on my life it's hard to decide whether I have great courage or great foolhardiness. I leap forward with total trust, I do always have faith and gratitude lots of the latter, sometimes not clearly seeing the road ahead it's a case of step forward and have faith in my gut feeling. As the ancient mystic Rumi said start walking and the road will appear. Always in life I have walked forward with total trust of being cared and provided for by the universe, I only have a bit of a problem when things don't happen at once my inclination is to paw the ground a bit, all arrives in my life in the right place and at the right time it's just a test for my patience.

As a friend said, we ask for apples and receive a banana but often we don't recognise it, as we didn't realise that a banana was what was really wanted at that time, the trick is recognising when a banana comes along that it's for us.

After staying with friends for a couple of weeks, the autumn came and I managed to persuade the builders to let me live in the new extension, being built onto the side of the old barn. Work on the old part of the building was still to be started, so I just moved in and camped out in the hall, bedroom and utility room.

I could put up with anything just to be reunited with my beloved Dillon and Max.

Slowly the older part was put together around me. When the builders left for home at night, the CD player was set up on the upper floor in the large space of the barn; an upright chair was then placed in the middle of the room on a large piece of board that I had laid upon the joists. The three of us Dillon, Max and I sat there by candlelight until late at night playing Bach or Philip Glass at full volume. It was like taking a shower in music, this wonderful thing can be done at any time as there are no immediate neighbours, I just let music pour over me and revive me, a home at last.

For so long I had been deprived of all the things that were so important to my life one being my deep physical need for music, this now is becoming clearer for me to understand the relevance of music on the body. It works it's healing by subtly altering the vibration levels, using certain sounds and rhythms it can alter the breathing lowering the breath to belly breathing, breaking the ungrounded habit of using just the upper lungs, this in turn helps to achieve a solid connection with the planet. So many of us have trouble with grounding and with incarnating here, me being just one of many.

Grounding has always been my main problem, it has taken me half a lifetime to decide to stay on this vibration level, as staying here has always been so appallingly, overwhelmingly, painful for me but there is much improvement, I am not alone with this problem it's very common, it's because we all know deep down that none of this is really real, there is always the underlying knowledge and a hankering to go home. But, as we are here for the duration of the current dream, we need to ground and one of the easiest things to counteract this problem is to take up gardening, put your hands in the earth and be your own lightning rod.

Soon the builders were finished and the first winter solstice was to come along. I celebrated this by myself, sitting with the dog and cat and for the first time bringing in the evergreens and lighting candles in the new house. Solstice was here and the candles have been lit many times since. To celebrate the Solstice is always important, it is also good to light a candle in the evening; it's a simple ritual that centres me wherever I am, connecting me with my friends in all dimensions.

The flame is a symbol of ongoing life. Rituals are good for us, so remember each evening as darkness comes in. to light a candle.

One day in the early winter I was sitting at the head of a long marble table that I had just set up in the garden, the marble had travelled with me for many years originally it was from a fishmonger in the East End of London, I looked around thinking that this was to be a special place where predominately female friends would come to meet. It was a place for them to provide mutual support and nurturing for each other.

They soon arrived, the first walked up to me when I was in a café, she told me that she had left home that morning, on a hunch and knew that she was to meet up with a new friend in the café. One after the other they all turned out to be healers, of many types, in time males turned up as well as females they are all very welcome, the energies of this house just attracts them.

Some friends move on to other countries and some remain, always new one's turn up and take their place at the table. The house is full of the most wonderful people and they're nurturing energies, given the amount of work that goes on here it's a remarkably calm building. Often I have found that when troubled people come to me its necessary to ask them to leave their emotional baggage outside the door, the building also needs energetically clearing regularly to retain its high vibrational level of healing energy, it's as important that the energy of a house is looked after and cleared as often as our own is.

Within two years of moving in a very sad day arrived when Dillon, my last wonderful wolfhound, friend and companion who was only three years old, one Saturday morning was found to have bone cancer. I had to take the decision to have him put to sleep the following Friday, on Sunday morning the day after the news of his illness had spread, a remarkable woman came to my house she was sent by a mutual friend. The woman was a dog whisperer she had walked around the village asking where the giant dog lived, she walked in the door looking just like a Botticelli angel and told me that she worked with disturbed children and animals and that she needed to communicate with Dillon to ask him what he had to tell me before he went. This was to be a skill that she, in turn, taught me or rather re-taught me and I have used it many times since, in fact almost daily.

It was an appalling week I stayed in the house and just lay on the floor with Dillon all of the time. Death and the grief was never so overwhelming as when John had died; I was too numb — that is the way it is — it comes out with the next death. Dillon had told the dog whisperer that he saw me as two people that were not in the same place— so even he saw me as ungrounded. He also told her that we had made the arrangement before we came together in this lifetime, he was only to stay with me for a short while to tide me over the worst time of John's death. Out of all the wolfhounds that have ever shared their life with me I loved that one so much, he was so caring and so attentive, dogs truly are the teachers of unconditional love.

After John had passed there were somedays when I would sit on the sofa in deep grief; Dillon would come up behind me and blow in my ear to amuse me, and then swipe a big woolly arm around my neck, I have cried into his wonderfully smelly woolly coat many times. For about a year after he had passed, he was at the door to meet me, either when I had been out late at night, or on returning after a few days away, or even just out shopping, on entering the front door on my return, in his energetic state he would press and lean against me, he will be there to greet me when my time comes to pass over.

Dillon said that my life will change and a dog would not work out with the future type of life that was for me, this proved to be true. The week after Dillon's death the next blow came; Max the cat very rapidly developed a kidney disease and had to be put to sleep as well.

With this second event I was sharply reminded that I had gone up the hills on a visit to a very energetically special land, owned by a good friend, on the land was a spiral, and I performed the ritual of walking the spiral, my request had been that my guy ropes be cut, as freedom was something I wished to experience. Yet again I am constantly reminded and warned of the energy that I put into my manifesting, and that care must be taken to think carefully before acting, impetuosity for me is a bit of a problem.

A few months after Dillon and Max's death my seventieth birthday supper was held in the garden. A small black kitten came in and played under the table with everybody's feet, she belonged to a neighbour, and now pops in every day to see me, in the winter she lies in front of the lit wood burner, there we go, this way I've landed up with the best of both worlds a cat that has other owners, this gives me the freedom to come and go to wherever and with whoever calls at a very short notice.

Try hard to communicate with all animals, whenever it is needed, or just in passing, it's so easy. Recently I had a wonderful example of this, one day a beautiful butterfly was caught in an old spider web, on my approach the butterfly panicked, so silently speaking to it and explaining what was needed, I asked it to remain very still, whilst the web was carefully unwound with the aid of a twig, It calmed and stayed completely motionless on my hand, when free it flew up into the air, circled around my head then flew off, I watched it and realised that there is no barrier between our understanding of each other, we must just communicate, This was not the first time that I had contacts with a butterfly they are very special, they are messengers. I find that even so called "inanimate" things will be compliant when addressed with complete confidence, we just still ourselves, calm and align to the energies of whatsoever it is, be it a person animal, tree, flower or stone, all things are animate in their own way, all are just another manifestation of the greater source.

This was the start of a new and amazing life for me everything was and is such a surprise, and I do love surprises, you don't get many of those when you get a little older, you've seen it all before.

Life number two, here we go, I'm moving through it at such speed now as if my time is short and there is so much to be done, and with such joy that my super skateboard has more than oiled wheel's it has wings, a skateboard called Pegasus? Very suitable my ruling planet is Mercury and I was born in the year of the Horse, plus named Angela— one hell of a lot of wings around here to contend with — it's no wonder I get so ungrounded.

Chapter Three

> Hope is the fuel of progress and fear
> is the prison in which you put yourself
> TONY BENN

FIRST I think before we get lost that a quick run through of my life, number one, would be in order.

In this lifetime my birth was in Nottingham England at 6.30 on a wet Monday morning in September 1942. My delivery was performed by my grandmother — a midwife. I was to be the third child down in the family. The first having had a different father than the rest of us, and the second child caused a rather rapid marriage.

Due to the bombing of London my mother Dorothy, myself and two older sisters were to spend the duration of the war in my mother's parents house, this resulted in the now enviable extended family. My father Robert was drafted into the eighth army and was serving in the desert. Not the most auspicious start in life, but I was loved and safe unlike many others at that time.

Grandfather Jack Oakes — Pop — was an ex-miner, local union leader and also a Labour councillor. Grandmother Ellen — Nanny — was a founder member of the women's branch of the Labour party and a dearly loved midwife; who in her time had delivered over three thousand babies into the world mostly in the Wigan/Hindly and Nottingham areas. She is known to have delivered three sets of twins in twenty-four hours single-handily, that's some lady. My much loved grandfather, Pop, wore old soft blue dungarees for daily wear, they were covered in patches that he had sewn on. The end of one of his fingers was missing; he told me it was buried in the churchyard and he would join it one day. His arms were covered with mining "tattoos" these resulted from a combination of cuts and coal dust. As a child, I was impressed by the fact that he had a very special suit that he called his going to meeting suit. Pop was always going to meetings, for the council for the Labour Party, or trade union meetings, for the miners, and also for the cricket club, the football club, and so on.

When Pop left the mine he became a window cleaner and would rise very early in the morning. Hearing him alerted me to run down the stairs and then sit on his knee so that way I could dip bits bread into the fat that came with his bacon sandwich. He was loved by me very much and I thought he was my father. Like many others, my real father, did not return from the war until I was nearly four years old. Pop and I were obviously both very early risers and dawn chatterers. After the dawn snack and world discussion with Pop, it was a quick jump back into bed, then rise with the others for the next breakfast sitting.

I was always hungry in a house of food, probably in another incarnation I was short on food. As a child I would steal food and sit in corners eating it. Yet food was readily available. A little later when my parents had a hotel in Brighton I was caught one time sitting on the back step rapidly stuffing into my mouth the hotel's whole cheese ration that I had just stolen.

As a very small child, whilst still living in Nottingham, a treat was to sit on the knee of Earnest Bevin for apple tart and a bedtime story. He was Minister for Fuel and was a regular visitor of my grandfather's, coming to discuss wartime coal mining matters. This was the way that politics and justice came into my life at a very early age indeed one might say in fact they were at every meal.

After the war, in 1946, when Father returned. We moved south to Brighton in Sussex where my parents bought a hotel, then some time later my grandparents upped sticks and followed us south for their retirement, resulting in an extended family to care for us all.

Beach House, a Regency hotel in Brighton, was purchased. The building was situated in a Georgian Square next to the sea front. The beach was so close, that life became one big adventure for the three of us, my two older sisters, Geraldine, Isabel, and me Angela.

At that time there was no culture of fear, children played for hours on the beach, streets or in the country side, only to return home at meal time.

Sunday mornings our father would walk us along the prom to Hove with us sneaking a look at the McGill bawdy postcards with all their brilliant stylised illustrations. Father walked in front with hands behind his back and we followed all dressed alike in navy-blue double-breasted overcoats — for me being the third down my coat was very much a hand me down. Given my parents sense of drama we must have looked good, including my parents, all of us were shades of red or blond. One of father's unfortunate enthusiasms was Aryan breeding; before the war he was a fan of the composer Wagner as well. Although all of these enthusiasms were fashionable then, they are rather embarrassing given there connotations now.

Left alone to our own devices we children came across many strange things and situations on the beach; one might say it was our school of life. On a beach stroll early one morning we found a very dead and battered man washed up by the tide. He was the first dead body I had seen. We stood there in a row and kept staring at a hole in his back.

Another day a violent gang of boys hit my sister Isabel around the head with stones. This was to be just the first of her many head injuries. It always seemed to be the head with Bell and the heart for me.

We were enterprising children even though pocket money was not something we really knew about. One day we three decided to take ourselves out for a cream tea, we walked to a café a long way along the beach. When we had ordered and were sitting waiting we realised that money was needed to pay for this cream tea, and we had none. So whilst the waitress left the room we ran home with our matching striped jumpers stuffed into our buckets desperate not to be recognised. Isabel, being the practical one organised all of this. She could only have been seven at the time with me just five. The freedom we had compared to the modern child would astonish people now. But when asking around my friends it was the same for many of my generation and not odd at all.

Just after dawn on the beach one morning we met up with Prince Monolulu, he was a famous bookmaker — betting took place on the race track then — he was taking a pre-race stroll and he gave each of us a sixpence. Me being five at the time, I was very impressed with this amount of money, rather than the fact that it was a very large, black African tipster dressed up with a feather headdress, who gave it to me, he would certainly not be able to give children money nowadays. He was in Brighton for the Kemptown horse races and used to shout "I gotta horse" when, as a bookie, he opened his book to take the bets.

So there we are. This was to be the start of a wonderful upbringing of benign neglect that was to serve us well in our highly varied future lives. Each one of us is totally different from the next. I'm sure this is down to the fact that our parents allowed us all to develop as we wished.

Father had been an actor before the war and he was also trained as a designer draughtsman. He had a good eye for paintings as well as an ear for music. My mother was a concert and opera singer with a thirst for politics and literature. She was a natural medium and was always reading someone's palm, working out their birth chart, or just giving them channelled information. This latter ability was passed on to her many offspring and helps to shape our daily lives and our view of reality.

Neither of my parents had subjects that were off limits and all questions were answered with enthusiasm; nothing and no thoughts were off bounds. We were never belittled and were always heard out, everything was up for discussion. Life was full of books and music, and with me a precocious early reader, I almost ate books. How I wish those eyes would come back to help me do that now.

Father, being a bit of a philosopher, was always delving into some new religious thought or theory. So we had no conventional religion in our childhood. The only religion I remember was a short spell at the Christian Science Church on a whim of my mother's, she thought that the people who attended the church looked prosperous, and it might rub off. Well, that was a daft idea as it was not the religion that made the congregation prosperous it was the fact that they all came from solid middle class backgrounds. Other than that one aberration there were no holds bared on any type of philosophical thought they were all taken on and thoroughly if not boringly examined discussed and later cast aside, for another new idea to take its place.

Today I teach workshops on metaphysical self-healing, and when coming across people attending my workshops who have had a conventional, restrictive religious upbringing I see that it can act as a fetter to their development, it can instil a fear of thinking for oneself, they are always looking for the rules — are we allowed to think that will we be struck down.

Well there simply aren't any rules and that's it.

So there we are what better upbringing could we have? We were not pushed at school our parents said if we wanted to learn we would do so when we wanted to and that way it would be with enthusiasm. This was all very well but I don't think anybody really thought about me and why I was having difficulty with writing words and with getting my letters the right way around. Nobody realised that I was dyslexic. As I said, I still have difficulties with my writing and spelling to this day.

Whilst living in Brighton my next sibling Adrian was born, he was mentally and physically handicapped. This was owing to my mothers discreet nature of not informing anyone when she was pregnant, she had received strong drugs for a bout of pneumonia she had whilst expecting Adrian.

On arrival Adrian was a lovely boy and, although born with physical and mental disadvantage, he is a sensitive and also sees and hears things which the rest of us miss. He has often given me or his other brother and sisters a message, When Josh, my son, was just a young boy Adrian kept telling me that he would be on a big wooden boat. This was later to be true as Josh grew up to build and sail in an old replica boat.

Chapter Four

> Ancora imparo
> Forever learning
>
> Leonardo de Vinci

IN my house now there is a piece of paper pinned to the wall in front of my desk. Written on it, in Latin, are the word's ANCORA IMPARO. This was one of the first direct messages that my guides sent to me. It was in Latin as they so often are nowadays, so I went onto Google to translate it's meaning it is: "Forever learning" It had been written on one of the artist Leonardo Da Vinci's last drawings. He too was dyslexic and that fact brings me great joy as now, at last, in recent years the amazing talents and capabilities of dyslexic children are being recognised.

How very true that phrase has turned out to be for me. I never stop learning, always taking on new things, whatever it is just bring it on and hurry up as life is short. Often messages will come to me in a clear statement, or a clear line of writing, that can be seen in front of me. Sometimes it is carved in stone. At other times it is in one of my amazingly clear dreams, I experienced a wonderful dream a few years ago before reluctantly starting this extra life, but that will all be explained a little later.

In the dream I was sitting by a river with my friends, when three men in suits approached and called to me. They were carrying a cushion raised high in the air. I never did see what was placed on it. They then stepped forward and asked me to become the Queen of Portugal. Laughingly my reply was "Don't be silly". They returned and asked me again. The answer was "No try that lady over there she might want to". On the third time they asked me I stood up reluctantly and said: "OK! but only if I can wear jeans and a tee-shirt and never have to wear stockings and a skirt". All of this was conducted in Portuguese, a language not familiar to me. On waking, I gave this dream a lot of thought as it was obviously sent to me as a clear message. I then realised what its meaning was — OK! I can and will do whatever is asked of me by my guides, but it must please me first and be what I want to do as well. In other words I will do it my way.

This was a powerful message for me to remember as there is a tendency for me to jump in and say yes to everything suggested before having time to think "Do I really want to do this" or am I just being over enthusiastic and thinking of other's and not myself first? As a person "no" is not an easy thing for me to say. I hate to disappoint anyone or say "I'm sorry I don't want to do that". It won't make me resentful but it will make me close down and become unhappy. This is probably a female thing as from birth girls are programmed by society to please others, as a child we received rewards if we smiled and look pretty. We must all investigate this tendency and remove it. Why should we put aside our desires in exchange for another's? We don't need to dominate just learn to be equal and value our needs as much as the needs of others, I have a clear memory of a 1920s song that accompanied keep fit classes after the war, it went, "Keep young and beautiful, it's your duty to be beautiful, if you want to be loved" That song was outrageous, the message being that you obviously were never going to be loved if you were shapeless with stringy hair and buck teeth, and that the only beauty that was needed, was going to be the physical. Save us from the constant acidic drip of belittling females, the frightening thing is that females constantly do this to themselves as well as each other.

It was in Brighton, around the time when Adrian was born, that I started nursery school and soon realised that I was not the same as the other children. I was a loner for starters and just liked to be myself and never to copy the way the other girls dressed or what they did. I was shy with a fear of rejection.

Well, that's not easy, being a loner in a big family! I was always stumping along independently, invariably winging about something, being too hot, too cold, hungry or too tired. I'm probably still the same now as I am incredibly sensitive to my surroundings, people, food and temperature, in fact anything in this world. It feels as if I arrived here with a layer or two of skin and a filter or two missing. The story of the princess and the pea has nothing on me! This tendency to being sensitive was something I learnt early on to keep hidden as it's a bore for other's.

Little did I realise until later in life that it is this very sensitivity that is the gift, that enables me to do the things that are needed to be done in this world; I easily link up with all things, animate and inanimate, their energies so fluently coming in and out of my body that is so extremely porous and very kinaesthetic, it was important to learn swiftly how to protect myself from the casual hurts inflicted on me without intention, also to learn how to control my embarrassing directness. I was under the impression as a child that all this was the norm, until, when starting school, I was rapidly disabused of the idea, with school came the start of the teasing. Also, the childish ganging up with unjust accusations, the latter still zooms me back to other lives of punishment, with accusations and stoning to death.

After nearly a lifetime I now understand from my guide, that it was part of my request to have the gift of dyslexia as well as being a right brainier, we do make our own plans remember. This type of brain enables one's understanding to be far more fluid in its problem solving abilities, because it's comfortable having to work very fast and free. Anything goes, there is nothing that it won't poke at and take on board. This type of brain is like a house without internal walls. You step in the front door go strait to the answer, but don't know how you got there. The "normal brain" goes through each room logically to reach the answer.

But just still ask me even at my current age to spell my name correctly or read the clock the right way around and all can land up in a mess. I still mix my b's and d's but that's OK, for me it is certainly no longer an embarrassment, also thank goodness for computers, though my life is a fight with them because they are so dumb, they just don't understand me.

A great enhancement to my life is a very close friend who has accompanied me through many previous lives, although the same dyslexia as me, the brain is brilliant, but when asked to do any normal thing that might want turning around or inside out and upside-down and they become rooted to the spot. Some days our conversations can be hilarious because they are full of dyslexic mistakes and spoonerisms, we just love jumping subjects at lightning speed and playing with words, this friend is the only possible person to edit this book as our brains work in a very similar way.

Unlike any other siblings that came before or after us, Isabel, my next sister up from me, and I started getting the most amazing series of life threatening illnesses. Luckily at this time my handicapped baby brother Adrian had a nanny, although how she was paid for is a mystery to me, she also looked after us in conjunction with my grandmother who had come south to stay for a while before her final moving in with us. It was then aged around four years old, that my life changed, I found out not everyone in life is to be trusted. My sister Isabel had pleurisy at the time and has forgotten but must have been temporarily sleeping in my grandmother's room when in crisis. Consequently I was left to sleep in the front basement bedroom on my own.

The family were very busy running the hotel, Isabel's illness and the new baby Adrian's, disability. Possibly nobody noticed or was caring for me as well as they should have been. We can all be judgemental in retrospect.

There were maids who worked in the hotel and slept on the top floor. One of the maid's boyfriends, having a liaison with her, would creep in through my bedroom's previously unlocked sash window late at night, on his way to creep up to the top floor. He would bring me an orange or banana as a treat, these fruits were very rare then as the war had just finished. My memory of him is very clear; he had dark hair and would sit me on his knee and sexually interfere with me, telling me not to say anything. I was between four and five years old at the time.

I had never told my parents from an overwhelming sense of guilt and fear of being bad — not really good enough to be loved. This feeling followed me through life but I did not recognise where it had come from for a long time it was completely buried until much later in life.

Often the thought of this abuse popped in my mind — such as who was that man who got me out of bed in the night and gave me fruit and why so secret? It just seemed a repeating odd thought. It was for this reason that I was unaware of the answer when asked some time later about my lack of virginity. Thinking it odd I did not understand the reason I was not curious and had no explanation as to why this should be. Such memories are buried so very deeply where they are safe and are hidden from hurting, wrapped in our unconscious like a grain of sand in a pearl.

My memories of this abuse were totally repressed for many years only to surface much later. They were disturbed by the release and balancing of the heart chakra, with its inevitable clearing of this life, plus past life memories and blockages, new ones still come up for clearing, that's OK. Just let them go. I now realise that, the abuse was probably just a trigger as it was in this life that I chose to clear deep hurts, from previous lives.

Clearing my heart chakra was just part of the process that I was undergoing, we all need to travel light and clear old junk out to make space for the future.

As we vibrate with energy, and actively clear and align with different levels where we are comfortable we can develop clear communications with our guides and teachers. As individuals clear so the people around them both before and after them clear. Remember our total connectedness, so with the general rising of the vibrational level there is no way to stop this acceleration, or suppress the knowledge of ancient damage surfacing for accepting and processing.

So this way, it was inevitable that the child abuse came to my conscious mind later in my life, when working on clearing and healing the emotional as well as the physical heart. This by itself is a painful and uncomfortable process at the best of times, it is a reason why many refuse to go forward in their personal development the unknown holds fear, in one life or another we all do it, its inevitable, we are all in the process of developing to our full potential, we all get there.

To be sexually assaulted as a small child cripples ones emotional response, it instils a constant desire to do the very best and to please everybody, the child feels guilty, when told that they will be in trouble if they tell anyone. It is hard to lose the sense of guilt even as a rational adult. Guilt forms a barrier of safety and an automatic rejecting response to anyone who comes in too close emotionally however much one would wish it otherwise.

Having since been told by many others that they have been in the same situation, and that parents and siblings often don't want to know, they say you imagined it, and sweep the abuse under the carpet, this attitude can't be tolerated, especially as we are now aware of the shocking statistics related to child sexual abuse, it having affected one in every five girls, that alone means that we all unwittingly know of a few, amongst our friends and acquaintance. To lose the sense of guilt we must all bring such things out into the open to be acknowledged, without embarrassment, and learn to love ourselves, and say that it had happened to us as well as to others, then forgive ourselves and the person who perpetrated the crime — because it is a crime.

After childhood abuse, of any type, one builds a powerful barrier around the heart to protect it. As a child, the heart is the only thing that is truly your own. It's easy to develop an innate distrust of people and of allowing them in too close; as if the splinter is still buried deep in there. So it has often been hard for my wonderful friends to dig me out, but the outer wall is only of clay and the true ones are good at spade work and just march in and leave the door open.

I am here in my eighth decade learning to recognise and repair the hurts to my body mind and heart emotionally and not just with the intellect. To accept and acknowledge something emotionally from the heart is much harder than only understanding what it was all about with the brain and intellect.

Although I am extremely self caring and loving now as an adult, when still a child after an early bad experience one can develop an unhealthy compulsion to put oneself into dangerous situations with unsuitable people of the opposite sex. Always something deep inside is doubting, and testing, as if you have to put yourself in a situation to be hurt again and again, to reassure something hidden deep that it did really happen, and it was not imagination, rather like a child picking at a scab to see if it still bleeds.

I had no understanding of my behaviour then, but thank goodness for my early marriage and being loved and cared for from aged seventeen years, otherwise it's sad to think what would have ensued. I was always running very close to the wind, always pushing the limits, always testing.

At fourteen, I would go out with gangs of much older boys on motorbikes travelling much too fast and doing stupid tricks with no helmet on. I remember being thirty miles away from home and racing on disused airfields, I found being alive was too painful, I wanted to hurt myself to feel, the pain physically.

It's only recently that I've repaired myself and decided to stay on earth for the full duration of this lifetime.

Although very tempted many times in my life to be casually intimate with others its usual for me to steer clear from fear of allowing another in to close this is due to a lack of trust i.e. I panic that way, I'm safer by myself and won't be hurt. I suppose that was what in my early youth, going out with much older men and drinking alcohol was about, it takes the edge of life and dulls the sensitivity, and thank goodness I have no problem in the alcohol direction now.

Although my Mother told me she did not like me behaving like I did, I wonder why she never asked me what it was all about. Probably I would not have had any words to explain my behaviour, so I just went on doing stupid things. My feelings are now so strong for that young girl who was me then, I want to hold her so close and make her safe and tell her that I will love her and protect her always. I never really trust that it is true, when people say they love me. I just can't believe that it still fills me with tears to think of that painfully fearful hidden child, who rebuffs everyone.

John, my husband, was the only one person who just casually stepped through all of the barriers I had carefully erected, but it was pre arranged before coming here into this life, he was seven years older than me he was so familiar and I felt totally safe with him. Early on in our marriage John learnt to call me whenever he would be late from work, because if he was ever late home without saying when he would return, I would be almost paralytic with fear sitting on the stair thinking that he was run over or had just died. I would convince myself that he was dead sitting almost physically doubled up with grief; even breath was difficult if he was not there. He was the only reason that I was alive.

He was around six feet tall and very sturdy. I never told him really what my thought's or feelings were for him as they were so painfully overwhelming. He gave me the impression of a calm solid stone, Doric column standing just behind my shoulder rooted as deep in the ground as he was tall. Being a Scorpio his feelings were secret. He was my anchor and kept me rooted to the earth by the very physicality of him, he was a person with four corners.

Until recently I viewed life as a prison sentence, never wanting to be alive, only really truly being here willingly in this dimension since my recent brush with death, after driving the car into a tree as a bee distracted me.

My spiritual guide communicated with me concerning the occasion, saying that there was a choice for me to either go through the gate or stay in this dimension, I decided to stay and step forward whole heartedly to take up the mantle of my true vocation, now I enjoy everything life has thrown at me. Since that accident my awareness of my guides love and support for me has been very reassuring. I realise my guardians have worked overtime all my life constantly protecting me so I thank them.

I forgive all who have injured me in the past including the man who abused me. He was probably unaware that he had set up a lifetime of reverberations. This stuff is disturbing to write? but putting it onto paper takes away its power, far better that, than for it to be swept away and say it's of no significance. Just put it out there and stand by all the other females in the same position. It was not our fault. We were not to blame, we are not bad and we can be loved.

Chapter Five

Some of the brightest minds in the country can be found on the last benches in the classroom

Dr Abdul Kalam

WELL — after that digression — back to the family. Living in Brighton at Beach House Hotel was a success. Now the war was over people were taking holidays and our family was still growing — it went on increasing to another two with Julian and Celia. Life might have stayed that way forever: an idyllic upbringing in the exciting seaside town of Brighton.

As is always the way in my life, just when things are settling down and I am enjoying where I am — bang! — and the world changes yet again.

My father was impetuous and impatient. He looked in an estate agent's window one morning and proceeded to fall madly in love with a Victorian mansion, it was surrounded by seven acres of gardens in the middle of the Sussex Weald. In the war the house and land had been requisitioned for housing evacuee children from the city's.

Father decided there and then to sell up and move us all to the heart of the country, to open another hotel. For starters, it was not a well researched move. In fact, it turned out to be a disaster. Petrol was still on ration and the house was well off the beaten track, possibly that was why the price was so inviting.

It was at this time after making such a disastrous move that life started to take a financial nosedive getting very hard for our parents. On the other hand it was all a wonderful adventure for us children and for me in particular, as now at last I was in the world of plants instead of stones — don't get me wrong I love stones as well. Life opened up with my first wonderful smell of the earth and plants. I just dived straight in and wow! I was five years old and the plants acted as a trigger setting me off working with them yet again, giving Isabel just the right ones to eat, so she ran to mother saying Angie's going to poison me, strangely enough they were the right herbs for her.

Being in touch with the earth brought all the old information back to me as nothing is ever lost. I understand now and know that many of my lives had been spent as a herbalist and a shaman with all their different names, some very derogatory. Many times, when you are a young child, other lives slip through very easily, up until five years of age children often slip into past lives as well as other languages. From that day on my whole life was spent upside down in the earth, I even had daffodils blooming in the snow because I took stone hot water bottles full of pebbles from the Aga and buried them deep in the snow around the flowers at night.

It was my habit as a young child to walk around with a toad or slow-worm in my pocket; they were my closest companions. On one occasion I caused my highly pregnant mother to jump through the bottom of a cane chair when I came into the kitchen and casually pulled a toad from my pocket.

I have a lifelong habit, perhaps brought through to this time from a previous life, that when I look at flowers that I have never seen before, I then often rapidly name them in Latin and know what they are for. I believe that sometime in a past life I must have been well-educated in botanical Latin. It's a strange paradox that I spell correctly in Latin but due to my dyslexia very rarely in English, as a herbalist all is so familiar to me that I almost feel like I am, cheating but I'm not. It's all my knowledge from many other lifetimes that comes back to me in this one.

It was when the family lived at Oakdown that the time came for the start of my formal schooling. The memory brings tears to my eyes even now. Why should memories of school be so painful? Attending school should be a time of adventure. I went to a small, two room village school with a coke stove at one end, the teacher stood with her back to it toasting her heavy tweed skirt after the rain, I could smell the scorching wool and the smell of it, it is still with me. It's a bit like the smell of wet dogs. The teacher was very nasty to me and constantly poked me in the back with her pen for persistently writing back to front and having an innate inability to spell even my name twice in the same way. For starters the name "van der Schuit" was not the easiest name for a dyslexic to be hampered with. The term dyslexic was not in use at that time so I was poked with a pen instead. I often wonder how many people were "cured" of dyslexia by pen poking?

Although writing legibly was not my thing, I was a very early and avid reader, spending hours sat in the under stair cupboard with a pile of National Geographic magazine. My brain's a bit free-range and wanders all over the place. Nothing was or is too complex to investigate. Today I thank the gods for the modern computer! I also thank my writing helpers from other dimensions they are always available to help me and enjoy participating, putting their bit in and having a general jolly, whenever we sit down to write. One's guides just love being asked to fully participate in your life.

Well, there we were living in a very large mansion with extensive grounds, the biggest house for miles about, but the time rapidly came when our dresses were to be made from the flowered curtains and we each took a sack to search for wood or coke to keep the Aga going. We were almost penniless, shoes were the hardest thing, we three girls were dressed the same and though that's been said before, it was no fun as being the third one down as life got a bit boring on the clothes front.

My strongest memory is of always being dressed in navy gym slips with a felt or straw hat, a bit like an extra from St Trinnian's. It was my habit to wear a wreath of oak leaves around my straw hat. My shoes were on the wrong feet for many years or I had put my eldest sister's drooping navy school knickers on by mistake. Mother said that whatever she did I would always look like an orphan.

All of this though was not so surprising as clothing then was far more complicated and one needed to know one's left from one's right. Brown strap shoes — on the wrong feet — beige lisle stockings that sagged into wrinkles around the ankle, a liberty bodice with rubber buttons on the bottom to hold the stockings up, baggy knickers to the knee with a pocket for a damp hanky, a scratchy serge box pleated gym slip tied around with a sash, plus a double-breasted navy overcoat all topped with a round felt hat, and in the summer a straw one. Getting dressed was a long and complicated affair.

It was at this time, that I was very jealous of my sister Isabel. This was because when I was young, my hair was a thick, frizzy, bright copper colour, cut in a pudding bowl style with a crooked fringe — probably because I squirmed in protest when it was being cut. This cut was a way to control my hair, but on the other hand Isabel, at one-time had big, fat, shiny chestnut ringlets with a perfect satin bow. How I wanted a satin bow so much, one day when we were walking down the street a person asked her if she had her little brother with her — I was mortified.

That must have been the start of my aversion about going to get my hair cut as I am only happy and feel like me when it is in a mess, by preference doing its own thing. My hair is the symbol of my still strong femininity, and refusal to conform. Possibly too I'm aware also that it is only now at this time in history, when one is into ones eighth decade, that one can still be accepted on all levels as a female with all the same vital energy and sexuality. One never changes with age; we are the same, just with a few wrinkles, a bit like an elderly car with a few dents and scratches.

Although my hair is not grey and given my colouring never will be, I cheer whenever I see an older woman with long curly silver grey hair, I cheer that the hair police have not nobbled her, no longer is it necessary to sport the she/he short haircut of the older woman, to step back and to sink into a neuter role and take to wearing beige or peasant black. For goodness sake take on a lover, take up skydiving, just walk out of the door and do what you always wanted to do; whatever turns you on, but do live the whole of your life.

Love everyone and everything thing that you do — do it with great passion right up to the finishing post. Never ever sit down and wait death's arrival and never regret what you didn't do. Never think of retirement just think of it as having an allowance that subsidises what you are doing next. I find that the older I get the more I am liberated from ties and conventions, not that they ever got much room before!

There is also no chance of me being confused with a boy now as there are far too many miscellaneous curves to contend with. That last thought brings a wonderful recollection from my youth. It was my father's rather tactless comment to me at thirteen years old, he gazed at me as I was washing up one day, saying, "You are just like a Renoir now", Oh! how romantic I thought, "... but in time you will look just like a Reuben's." I'm confident that someone loved Reuben's beauties even if it was only him.

We can all only be the end result of those that genetically came before us, however much we try to change ourselves in our youth. We will still land up as the copy of an ancestor, mother, father, or great aunty Annie; one of those that came before us. All your thoughts and beliefs are filtered through your body so be very careful about what you think about yourself, remember that you did choose this body and this place for a reason and to encourage yourself not to put yourself down. Our bodies are just on loan and like cars we need to love and care for them or they will breakdown and ditch us one day, just when we least expect it.

As *The Management* like to regularly remind me, look after your vehicle — your body — and remember to take a rest every now and then, and do have FUN. Oh! there's that word again.

Chapter Six

> Don't go where the path may lead;
> go instead where there is no path and leave a trail.
>
> RALPH WALDO EMERSON

As houses went, Oakdown was amazingly haunted. This often happens when a building is erected on a place of crossing energy lines, i.e. Lei-lines. We children just accepted the other worldly residents as normal. Though I did ask when quite young if I could be excused from seeing them please, just knowing that they were there and hearing and seeing them in my head were enough for me. Seeing other dimensional presences is still not easy, often my clairvoyant abilities are weak but certainly I can feel and hear them. I'm always surrounded by my many Spiritual helpers and teachers. To start with they show me what they look like by putting pictures in my head and that's OK, to live with, as they become familiar the human picture fades, I just don't want to bump into any otherworldly presences unexpectedly. Feeling the sudden electric shock when my guides are close is enough for me.

One day in the distant past I did have a rather electrifying experience when working in what was originally a large private house at the corner of Hanover Square in London. I was running down a flight of spiral stairs at speed when I ran right through the middle of a person who was not in this dimension. It was like getting an electric shock. I automatically turned to apologise to them but just saw the fuzzy, electric blue outline of someone ascending the stairs.

Isabel, my sister, has always seen lots of those who have passed on. One of her best childhood ones was our great-grandfather on the Dutch side of the family. He had a red beard and sat on her bed wearing a sou'wester. The departed like to show themselves to us in a relevant manner and in a form or age which is meaningful for us even suitable for when we are a child. Some years later, when looking through old photos one day, we found a picture of him in his Sunday best. We looked at him through a magnifying glass and were astonished at how a face continues, in this generation his nose and brow is the same as mine. His name was Benedictus and Isabel must have been special to him as he always kept her company when she was ill. We think he is still around her now when needed.

In the bedroom that Isabel and I shared, there was also another entity but unrelated to us. She was a tall woman who sat at her mirror putting on a hat with many layers of veils. My mother told me that she was the original owner of the house who had long ago died of throat cancer.

What intrigues me is why do these often meaningless visions of the past remain? Was the moment so meaningful to the person that they left an imprint?

There was one occasion of encountering an energetic imprint that I do understand. It was when we were on our way home from a holiday in Scotland. As we drove along a road it was a sunny day and all was happy. Suddenly I felt a doubling up feeling of total gloom and despair that was so overwhelming. We stopped the car to take a break only to discover that we were driving along the edge of the Culloden battlefield. Now there's an event that will have left its vibrational mark; a place of great brutality and sadness where up to two thousand men, mostly Catholic Scots and fifty, mostly English, government soldiers were killed. Culloden was one of the bloodiest battles and the last pitched battle to take place on British soil.

My life certainly contains many other entities from different vibrational levels now. As they themselves put it to me one day, I have a plethora of helpers around me, to aid me with my work. They use such a wonderful mixture of words, sometimes so grandiose and at others almost trendy. For instance on the same days as they informed me that I had a veritable plethora of helpers, they also asked me to start a JV. Well, that was mystifying to me until it was explained that a JV was a *joint venture* — a newsletter and perhaps to start one with friends contributing.

This JV was to be the start of *The Cross Quarter Day News*, a newsletter to connect friends who are all healers in their many guises, so they can inform all friends and clients of their latest news and donating a short article concerning their ideas and current workshops.

My guides and helpers are with me every day, often in the night as well, the latter is an easier time for them to connect with me, sleep is when the brain stops racing with the ego in charge. When we sleep we dream and dreaming time is a time when we are able to receive a lot of information.

We all of us have personal guides, helpers and guardians. The amount of these increases as we request more of them, to work with us. They help with whatever we are trying to achieve in this dimension, when manifesting a dream, or project that aligns with our highest intentions, and accords with the path that we selected before we arrived on the earth.

The majority of us are brought up in complete ignorance of all the help and care that awaits us whilst we are here and find it hard to comfortably communicate with our guides and helpers. Our ears of intuition are closed, "We are simply untuned to they're prompting" To start with it is normally just a little nudge of intuition. They are with us for the whole of our lives, just waiting in the background. We chose who we want to help us on the trip into this dimension, all are chosen whilst at the planning session that took place long before we came to earth, It's all very mundane, there is no mystique. It's just how it is. We do have complete freedom to do as we wish whilst here on earth but it is much more rewarding to go with our birth intention.

Everything that I have written here has always been known, but has been obscured by the religion or superstition of the day. Over the centuries it gave our interceders a feeling of being special — *them* — having something *they* knew and we didn't. This gave *them* a feeling of superiority and power over people, because *they* are the chosen ones of the knowledge, creating separation, yet again, so that you needed *them* to access your *God*. All this is totally wrong. No human can come between you and your *God*, you go direct and it is immediate, we are all an aspect of *God*, never think that *God* and your guides are not there — when you ask they are. You are just not hearing clearly or are doubting, never doubt that they hear you and are always with you. There is no way that it is necessary for any other human being to intercede between you and your *God* or whatever you wish to call the source power. You are part of each other; you are a giant energy and the co-creator of your life never let people tell you otherwise. Beware of so called secret knowledge, there are no secrets; all is there to enable you to either access the innate empowerment and knowledge in your life or, shut yourself down, you choose, you are in charge.

There are many who will wish not to know, just to arrive in this dimension — *tabula-rasa* — slate clean. They wish to do it the hard way for a reason that is theirs to choose. One can't demand that people open their heart and eyes to become enlightened, each human develops at a different rate and at a different time, but they are all equal they will all get to the same place one day in one life.

Helpers from the other side can only wait and watch. They can't come forward to help unless we ask, so just ask, it is as easy as that. You will be amazed at who and what turns up, when following with a passion your true path, remember ask for more help and more will join you there are no limits on the helpers that you attract.

The whole concept is all too simple for us with all our baggage to comprehend. We think we are not worthy and we imagine we must say please and that we will try to be good. That's not needed because there is no judgement, we forget that life is very simple really, it is we who make the obstacles because we are sometimes afraid of success or putting our head over the parapet; forever thinking that if we stand up we will be judged. But who is in a position to judge us on any level no one judges us, there is not a big black book with ticks and crosses it is just us and our very loving guides and helpers, who are touching base yet again. Think of life as being on a skating rink learning to skate alone then returning to chat to friends on the side between each attempt. We must never fear because fear is crippling, it is restrictive and we are here to expand and experience joy and love. Though standing back until asked, our guides do intervene in an emergency that would seriously disrupt our life's intention.

John once told me of a serious incident that was averted in his life. It was long before we met and when he was in the R.A.F. on a bombing run with real bombs. One became stuck in the tube and an officer who nobody knew or saw getting on, or off the very small plane came forward and kicked the bomb through. John, as well as the other men, was convinced that the man was not there in this reality but came to save their lives. That was interventional emergency help. We all know of some incident similar in our own life.

Society makes so many barriers and puts us on a guilt trip from the start. Just think of the tiny baby coming into this world with its inherited DNA going back from both sides to the start of time.

Then strap a massive rucksack onto that child's back promptly load it with all our own and society's prohibitions, plus all our fears that are then dumped on top. We judge them from day one and tell them what they can and can't do, can and can't think; in fact all our rubbish. Children are often pushed at school to be something that we want them to be, something that we never managed to be. If only children were allowed to be a clean slate with none of our pre digested rubbish to wade through from the very start.

To go forward, the time has come when we too must take everything out from our own rucksack examine each thing and see if we want to walk through the rest of our life overloaded with excess baggage, slowing us down. Or do we just dump the bag stand up straight and do it our own way? Why wait until the next time you touch base here? Do it now, go forward and grow with your soul's desire, there is nothing and nobody to stop you, but you.

We have a need to learn unconditional love again, we had it on arrival as a baby, then everyone tries to steal it from us or we become disillusioned — we are told not to be so naive, for instance it's a real world out there, How about that one for cutting you down before you start, unconditional love is simple, learn to stop attaching strings to things and people.

Our ego is good at protecting us, but set it aside and communicate directly from the soul with love and forgiveness, that is first for yourself and then to others, make it unconditional and that communication will be direct to the heart of the matter. Only that way is it impossible to hurt or be hurt. Those who receive it as hurt are not yet in charge of their ego and allow it to get the upper hand in their emotional dealings with the world. The ego is here to keep us under the illusion that we are alive and separate and in fear, but in fact we are in a dream, after sleep you wake up from your dream in the morning and even though it was very real, by daylight it fades away. Life is the same its just a dream, and ego is trying to stop us from waking, as when we do and realise that we are not separate, but we are part of a whole, we are part of the greater source, with our realisation of this, the ego becomes redundant.

It is necessary to try to remember, never to tie strings of ownership or guilt on another. When you have a child you are the bow and they are the arrow, shoot the arrow as straight as you can, with no strings attached. Stand back and hope your love gets the arrow to wherever it needs to go. If you have done the best you can, allow the children to confidently walk their own path leaving them free and unhampered by the burden of pleasing parents.

We all have the choice to walk our pre planned path, but to succeed it must be walked with passion and determination or we will be sidetracked and give away our life and power to others.

Never ever lose your passion, it is necessary to feel our power rising through us from the ground beneath us. When united with our greater self we are giants in other dimensions, when here on earth we forget who we really are. We must not let society put us down and waste our opportunities, above all we must learn to expand with unconditional love, to be non-judgemental and have compassion for all people. Love is so life giving and empowering that's all that's needed, don't rush through life trying just to achieve, achieve, achieve as by doing so you may miss the opportunities to spread joy and love, remember that the journey is as important as the arrival.

Right, after that deviation let's go back to where we were again. Growing up as a child of nature, a loner in a large family, I was always rather a serious a child with a straight face and was called Lizzy dripping, a term of endearment used for a fey child in the north of England where my roots are. I was the sort of child who people in the street and shops would always tell: "cheer up it will never happen".

I still am too serious and my guides continuously tell me to have fun. Have you ever sat down and thought tomorrow, I will have some fun? It's a weird thought, nothing really comes to mind and it leaves you at a loose end, feeling a bit embarrassed. It's the same feeling that a dog gets when you ask him something he doesn't understand. He just gets up and sidles off looking a bit sheepish and apologetic.

As a child, my time was spent walking the country lanes, finding things for my nature table, chewing plants and lost in the joy of my surroundings. This is still a pleasure for me and I enjoy the changing seasons, taking early walks in nature, if the weather is on my side.

Whilst at primary school I discovered that my ginger hair always got me into trouble and was often called out in class by the teacher for being naughty. I was always the one teased at school with the call of "Oy, you ginger" and was always blushing. Now in my seventies I no longer blush and my hair is starting to go white, this will soon make me invisible — great as I can then get up to mischief.

So, there we are I was a fey and serious child, a loner.

Chapter Seven

Success is walking from failure to failure with no loss of enthusiasm

WINSTON CHURCHILL

WHEN I was seven years old Julian, my second brother, was born at Oakdown. The time had also come for my grandparents to retire and move south, to live with us. Pop took up work locally as a window cleaner and this helped support us financially, he was also always mowing the grass and growing the vegetables, we really needed his extra help, income and gardening skills. To this day I have a warm memory of lying inside the wigwams of peas munching away at the peas plus their pods, or standing at his side learning planting songs, whilst planting the vegetable seeds with him. I was the same as many wartime children who were brought up by grandparents, being that I really considered Pop to be my father.

Nanny was always in the kitchen making bread. My clearest early memory of her is of arms; plump and dimpled, belting hell out of bread, giving it a good knead, at other times I accompanied her in the garden picking plants. Nanny was very connected to herbs and my strongest memory was being at her side picking nettles for nettle beer that regularly exploded in the deep, dark pantry.

Nanny taught me many of the properties of plants. I still have a book that I wrote down her instructions for the treatment of gout. Herbal medicine at that time was still in regular use; a habit that hung over from people who were unable to afford the doctor before the onset of The National Health System, Nanny had also used herb's extensively in her practice of midwifery.

Now at last herbal medicine is being accepted as a viable, safe alternative to many of the allopathic medicines, with their multiple side effects. Herbs need to be administered with care by a trained person as they are not entirely harmless in untrained hands. Herbs are food writ large they have been proven by their use by us over a very long time. We must be vigilant and guard them well or they will all be banned or patented in time in favour of the major profit hungry pharmaceutical companies.

We lived for many years in Oakdown paying guests were few and far between. We did have one set of visitors though who were an enchantment; they were a troupe of pantomime performers. For a child this was absolute magic, as they taught us how to walk on our hands, and do cartwheels and somersaults as well. From that day it was always my habit to do a cartwheel on my birthday up until recently, after splitting the macula in the left eye in a car accident. Before the pantomime troupe left us, they gave us tickets to the show in Hastings — a wonderful event. Remember that television was not commonplace in 1950 only the butcher in our village had one that says a lot as it was just after the war so he must have done well for himself. Entertainment was a radio with valves that constantly needed soldering by Pop. Our high point prior to the pantomime trip was a lantern slide at the vicarage.

By this time Adrian, my disabled brother had progressed to walking about the gardens with his leg still in an iron calliper. As the garden was full of adders he was closely followed and under the strict guard of Bob our black retriever. It amazes me how our domestic dogs observe and understand more about us than we realise. Without instruction, they instinctively understand which of us need looking after and who our enemies are. Much as I adore dogs I have chosen not to have dogs now as I am not in the position to give them the attention that they deserve. I am now for the first time in my life free to go anywhere at a minute's notice. For the latter part of my life the dogs who were with me were Wolfhounds or Deer-hounds, I have had four in total and once you have lived with one of these breeds they are hard to forsake for any other breed. It's very hard now when I see one in the street I have to resist the urge to cross the road and hug them. Please don't let anybody bring a stray one looking for a home to my front door; I would have to take them in. I am a complete walk over where Wolfhounds are concerned, for some reason I find them irresistible.

The gardens at Oakdown fell away from the house in terraces. One had a tennis court that was not used much, although my mother had played tennis for her county as a girl, she had not had much time for tennis having a tribe of children and being forever pregnant. Geraldine, my eldest sister, was a good player she had learnt at school, the Tunbridge Wells Grammar School where she was a weekly boarder. Gerry was very academically favoured; a tall strapping girl who walked home down the long rhododendron lined drive on Friday night, whistling in the dark to keep away whatever might be in hiding in wait for her. This left Bell and I home as a pair. In fact our names got run together when being shouted for. Bell was a very bold child and climbed down from the bedroom window via the ivy. She would also terrify Nanny by shinning up the massive cedar tree on the lawn and calling to her from the top, she is still game for anything and would be at her happiest as a traveller.

I have never had a head for heights. I find it hard to watch a film on television with someone walking in a precipitous place without putting the soles of my feet and hands on the floor because they hurt so much. I get an overwhelming desire to jump. Recently I found out why this is. It comes from one of my previous deaths when I fell or one might say was pushed from a height to my death. This was in a Cathar lifetime when many jumped or were deliberately pushed to their deaths in a time of persecution — unwanted information has a habit of popping up in my memory.

One gets a very long term view of life, or as one might say lives, as one links with old lives — are they old or current? — which drift in and out of our consciousness. There are other deaths from a past lives that are rather a nuisance to me now. In one, I have been falsely accused and surrounded by people who stoned me to death. Another was from drowning by ducking. Water and swimming are things I've battled with for many years as I find it almost impossible to take my feet off the ground when trying to swim. In my imagination I can almost feel the wonderful sensation in my body of twisting and diving like a fish, I would just adore to swim. The sensation of my thoughts comes through to me very physically. But in the water I am totally paralysed when it comes to lifting my feet off the bottom of the pool, unless I am holding the side. When trying to swim, it is important for me to be in charge as well as grounded, if someone tries to help I panic. Bizarrely I find no problem in sitting on the floor of the pool at the deep end for a long time, or with fingers just touching the side whilst floating eyes closed face down with my head under water, I feel very happy about it as the outcome is my decision. So there we are, we keep some memories as protection and some just hang around.

As a child there was a mishap whilst I was pretending to be a gondolier I twanged up a big stick that became stuck in the bottom of a very deep pond I immediately dropped out of sight as I was wearing wellies at the time. Bell came to the rescue yet again. She has taken it on as her personal job in life to rescue me. I suppose older sisters always have that function passed on to them from the day they are usurped by the next one. It must be rather strange to be a single child as we are by our nature programmed to be surrounded by siblings.

Chapter Eight

Insanity is doing the same thing over and over again and expecting a different result

Albert Einstein

THE constant weaving in and out of our relationships is fascinating, each life we are here with many of the same group of people just changing part's as a troupe of repertory actors would whilst going from city to city. In one place one would be playing the sister the next the daughter the next the mother.

The same group of souls constantly reincarnating together with an occasional bit part or major lead coming in from the outside. It is for this reason that when many people come into our lives with great familiarity, we just take up from where we left off before. Perhaps we are there to finish something we started in another life that was cut short or to help each other and pay back a kindness from a past encounter. There are many of these encounters in my life in fact the older I am the more connections I can see, at times it might just be momentary event as we pass a person in the street and screech to a halt of recognition that is so poignant; but the link was from another time and another life.

Once I saw a past life partner as we were passing through a swing door in a shopping arcade in Ipswich above all places. The connection was so strong; I nearly rushed forward to hug him. He recognised me to and we saw it in each other's eyes. We just stopped momentarily stared at each other smiled and passed on our different ways.

At this time in my life I am surrounded by friends, most who resonate with me so powerfully from other lifetimes. It's all a matter of opening up to the many opportunities and happy serendipities of life and understanding the boundless connect-ability. There is nothing and no one that we are not connected to, humanity is just one creature; like ants who live in total unison. Hurt your neighbour and you hurt yourself; love your neighbour and you love yourself too, this applies to the man or woman next door and to the whole world as well. How many times must one say it before the light dawns?

From birth, we suffer from the barrage of restrictive untruths, a child's mind has endless possibilities. It has no boundaries. So we promptly fill it with all our passed down junk; working away like Chinese whispers until the original thought is long obscured. We then sit the child in a school. I wonder when the system of "school" in its formal form first came along. We sit them there and cram them with passed down information. But how much of this information is true? Better to let them walk through life assisting them to develop their undistorted ability to learn and observe for themselves when the time is right.

Often it's not wisdom that we pass onto to our children. It's a load of second-hand bigoted rubbish that we have not really examined, but just taken on verbatim from the generation before. Very little education is about freedom of thought. It's about conforming and control, step out of line, be an independent thinker and you become a threat when really you are an enhancement.

Albert Einstein said "Imagination is more important than knowledge. Knowledge is limited. Imagination encircles the world". But remember he was, like Leonardo Da Vinci, dyslexic.

We, or rather our parents, struggled on living at Oakdown for seven years or so. For us children it was endless days of fun with all the space inside and out and very occasionally people would pass through. I have a clear memory of looking over the landing banisters down into the hall at guests who were dancing the Valletta to music from a wind up gramophone with its thorn needles, they needed sharpening after every few records, but mostly the house was empty.

The limited staff we had at Oakdown were from the hotel in Brighton. They had travelled onward with us and continued to do so through more house moves in the future. I often wonder why they did, perhaps they were just sort of part of the family troupe or perhaps they were waiting for their wages.

Oakdown was on raised ground set back on a balustraded terrace overlooking the Weald of Sussex. It was large and built of grey stone with massive red brick barley sugar chimney stacks; these could be seen from miles around. The roof had fretwork white gables and at the front of the house was a white painted conservatory. The conservatory was filled with that wonderful warm damp smell. The floors were of terrazzo and an iron grille covered the channel for hot water pipes. At the far end were French windows through to a billiard room that in turn led onto a short corridor with giant blue and white Chinese pots, onward through to the generous hall with sofas and fireplace and then to a smoking room — all very much a Victorian period piece.

The hall was vast; the walls were panelled in oak with secret drawers in which we kept table tennis balls and such things. At the rear of the hall was a grand arch crossed by the staircase. Next to the stairs there was a studded green baize door through to the staff quarters. The vast kitchen had cockroaches that scuttled under the Aga and on cold days in the winter I would sit on a wooden stool and put my feet in the plate oven of the Aga to thaw them out. On the first floor were the major bedrooms, plus the nursery area that Bell and I inhabited until other siblings usurped us. Opposite the nursery was a staircase to the staff bedrooms. Mother told me not to sit on these stairs or I would die of pneumonia. So I promptly sat upon them as often as possible — why did I want to die of pneumonia? I was always trying to die, obviously a reluctance to be incarnated yet again.

At the front of the first floor was a music room with two concert grand pianos, one a Steinway and the other a Bechstein. One was my mothers and the other my father's. This was really over the top when there was not enough money to pay the electric bills or keep us in clothes. On the wall was a set of shelves with a display of coloured Waterford glass, not much of that survived though with a growing family playing football in the house.

Mother often played the piano to us when we were in bed. Golden Slumbers was the name of the piece I remembered best. I can still hear her voice to this day, a rich and resonant contralto that would make the hair stand up on the back of your neck. I have a far memory when, as a small child, she would lean over my cot on returning from giving a concert performance; there was the rustling sound of her dress and the bouquet of flowers wrapped in silvery paper. The sad thing was that mother lost her voice and for a couple of years it became just a whisper. This was the effect of stress and having too many children, both disrupt the hormone balance and that in turn depletes the voice. Her singing voice did return after the menopause and we would occasionally hear it whilst she was working in the kitchen making dinner, when cooking she always sang.

At the rear of the house was a large courtyard lined with fascinating stone sheds, workshops and wood barns. The house also had its own circular oast house in one corner of the yard the oast house was for drying hops to make beer. Viewed from the front of the house, and across the lawns hidden behind a mass of rhododendrons, were U shaped two storied stables with a cobbled yard a clock tower in the centre block and a large iron ornamental hand pump for water. The yard was surrounded by stables with staff accommodation overhead. It was to be here shortly after their arrival in the south that my grandparents set up home.

They arrived one day with all of they're wonderfully heavy furniture, one piece that I loved was a sideboard with a marble top, on which stood a blue and white china pot of pot-pourri. The whole place was permeated with the smell of Pop's pipe tobacco; the smell of "Three Nuns" tobacco haunts me still.

My grandfather, born into poverty, was put to work down the pit at thirteen. He was self-taught at the Miners Evening Institute and was widely read, had a wonderful taste for oil paintings, furniture, blue and white china and books and I still have some his books to this day. He loved to go to sale rooms and ferret about to see what he could find a set of history books or beautiful pieces of furniture.

Nanny had started her working life in the same way as Pop, at the age of thirteen she worked in the mill as a bobbin girl, she had continued with her part-time education then later trained at a hospital in the East end of London where she became one of the first qualified midwives. She returned home to work in Wigan there she met married my grandfather and later my mother was born. For many people in the industrial north education only continued part-time after the age of thirteen, boys worked the ventilation shafts at the pit, girls were small enough to crouch under the cotton looms and retrieve the dropped bobbins accidents were frequent with boys killed and girls scalped.

The majority of people now have no conception of the poverty that the people lived and worked in with the arrival of the Industrial Revolution, They worked so very hard for so little reward, bringing such prosperity to the country and to their employers. There was wealth that had never been conceived of before. The bosses built vast mansions on grand estates, but for the working people it was the beginning of industrial slavery on a massive scale, we think of slavery as black but must never forget it was white as well.

The people of the countryside who were independent weavers were swept into the rapidly growing cities with they're accompanying slums — the rookeries as they were commonly known. It was a place where families lived on top of each other in abject squalor, where the air was thick with smoke and dirt; which was far from the green fields and the original home of spinning dyeing and weaving. The coastal islands of Scotland are one of the few places where such home industry still thrives.

When people talk of slavery, they never really consider that we in Great Britain suffered slavery too. The working classes were looked upon as sub-human. There were very few bosses who were humane or had safe and caring working conditions. People worked for a very low wage in appallingly dangerous conditions, at time this changed the face of society and the health of its people, so much so, that by 1914 when they were needed to fight yet another war for their masters they were stunted tubercular and under nourished.

All this at a later time though would help to bring about the creation of the welfare state, and I am proud to say that my family were in at its creation, as both grandparents were strong Socialists and worked unstintingly to further the idea of the welfare state, with its code of justice and health care for the working man and woman, plus free education for the child.

Nanny worked in Wigan in the slump, a period when the workers were just laid off and discarded. People lived in conditions that we would find it hard to imagine now. On occasion, she was delivering babies in the dark, with just the torch from her bike as there wasn't any money for candles, or any furniture and just newspaper on the floor for a bed. If you had no furniture a box was emptied for the baby. Many babies died in the first year in these conditions. We forget that antibiotic's have not been around for long; they have only been with us since the Second World War, 1939-1945

I was born in the middle of the Second World War and nearly became part of the child mortality statistic by succumbing to the Diphtheria epidemic at eighteen months old. My mother had been nursing me around the clock and was taking a quick break by going down stairs for a cup of tea, whilst my grandmother took over my care. My breathing stopped with no hope of revival, so I was wrapped up and placed under the bed as was the custom at that time. Nanny went down to tell my mother the sad news, at that Mother promptly rushed up and shook me until the breathing started again returning me back to life. A little later when I was aged four the good turn was paid back to my mother, who at the time was in the crisis stage of double pneumonia. The doctor and my grand parents were around her bed awaiting the end when by all accounts I rushed in, jumped on the bed and shouted where was my tea? There has always been an imperative hunger that must be fed — now— as far as I was concerned. That demand helped to call her back to her responsibilities as a mother, so she turned the corner and returned to us. My, now long passed, mother is still with me every day to help me with my work and comfort me with adjustments to the many vibrational changes that were necessary to undergo whilst coming through into my new life.

The more we perceive and work in conjunction with our higher guides, the higher our vibration rate will become, because of the extreme connectability of everything. As our vibration level changes, we automatically affect the people around us, before us and after us.

Some days I feel my mother so close. She is always touching and patting my face. It makes me rather emotional as her love for me, is so close. My mother is not from the same soul group as me, we arranged for her to help me through the difficult transitions I was to go through, on the other side we live in soul groups, but when we incarnate here we often are with a mix of those from a close group as well as our own.

John my husband and I were of the same soul group. We are soul mate's, on the other side, we are always with a third soul a male much younger than us. Since John passed our third member came briefly into my life, being with him was not a comfortable experience but, however, it was an important learning one.

Being alive has always been a problem for me. In many previous lives I have been persecuted so my visit here was with reluctance. There was work to finish that was started in another more dangerous time. At that time I was persecuted for my skills of healing and using vibration energies, I had to hide my abilities then, but earth is now a much safer place for me to finish my work. In fact there is a strong probably that my return was only because John accompanied me for a greater part of the journey in this lifetime. He has all my thanks for protecting and caring for me leaving me in a place of safety, he loved and provided for me no one could have more.

Chapter Nine

When life is rough, keep on walking
and the page will turn

Angela Baker

MY early brush with death at eighteen months was not to be the last by any means. Not that death has any fears for me, as my remembrances of other lives and other connections are so strong that this trip to earth is just one more short intermission in the real thing. This life as all the other lives are just a fleeting dream, we never die just move on to a higher vibrational dimension, when there we have no need for such a dense body. This world is such a dense place energetically and it is here that we live a Karmic existence; we keep on trying things out and learning, we can only reap what we sow and that is what we learn.

Being on this planet helps the soul to develop as it experiences all the choices available, some of these choices amaze us as we do not understand them, i.e. who would wish to be incarnated paraplegic, but if you think about it, that does provide a place for stoicism and unconditional love, both for the cared for and the carer, all situations have opportunity for the soul's development. The soul has a desire to develop, continuously moving up the spiral to a place of higher vibration, eventually becoming a very small part of the universal power of all things, with a complete loss of individuality — ego — in other words part of the whole.

I am constantly amused, when overhearing people saying "Go on give it a go, you only live once". They are just parroting things that they have heard others say; we are here to question everything. Try as I might, it's impossible to understand the arrogance of people who imagine that they are the perfected end product and that's it. We are here for multiple lives; there is no beginning and no end. But take a breath and remember that's the way they wanted their life and beliefs to be, it's not for me to get cross. One must try very hard to never judge and that is never easy task if one is a human.

One day understanding the conundrum of whether our lives are concurrent or consecutive will arrive. I must put it on the shopping list of things to ask *The Management* as my guides are affectionately called. It's a matter of great interest to me, as time is a fiction and only applies to this world and in this dimension. All things are in the here and now. All things are possible. All things have or have not happened at the same time. This is the view of quantum physics that is currently held, but we are still in our infancy concerning this subject. We probably live many of our lives simultaneous; when she met me in the flesh for the first time, an extraordinarily intuitive long distance friend of mine just stared and stared at me and told me that she saw hundreds of faces flashing across mine and she knew most of them. At that moment my face had one side that was very young and beautiful while the other was very old and wrinkled but the centre was extremely voracious in its constant thirst for knowledge —well I found that was a bit in my face to put it mildly. She sat and stared at me incredulous and said "You really don't know who you are, do you?" My reply was "Err, no, and I'll pass on that one", it's better not to know at this stage as I'm a bit busy with all the jobs they have sent me.

> *Once when walking on unknown land for the first time, in this life, I realised that I'd walked on it centuries before in another life and had a deep knowledge of just where I was. I saw myself as an adult walking on the slope of grass across from where I stood, the me on the opposite side was holding a child's hand and following a group of cows,*

just as always when daily walking that path in times past. Seeing myself as both the adult and the child I was simultaneously feeling the touch of the adults skirt fabric between my fingers as I clutched onto it, even though at the same time I was the adult and I recognised both the fabric, colour, and texture of the clothes, I also knew my name from that time, it was Alvera. I looked across, she smiled and waved to me through the dimensions and times. Holding her bucket high in the air she said the water was good. So I was there in that moment as three people who were all the same person in the same place in this dimension and we were all aware of each other.

Well, work that one out or just live with the thought that all things are possible. Once the brain is released from the straitjacket, we strap it into. This is not a very comfortable feeling, it's not exactly tea and biscuits on Sunday afternoon, that's OK, don't panic. It's just the stretching sensation of a brain expanding opening its doors into the endless enfilade — a vista of open doors — of the possibilities of quantum physics. Nothing is fixed except our perceptions of what things should be. Its time we stopped thinking that we are at the pinnacle of human development we are just at the first step of many. Learn to release the ego brain; open up the blinker's that we give ourselves to keep us feeling safe.

Right, now back to the main theme. The idyllic life we children had at Oakdown was to draw to a close rather rapidly. My parents, seeking out the possibility of selling up and moving on to pastures new, became involved with a trickster and forger and the situation landed up as a major court case held at the Old Bailey. At that time the forgery was impossible to prove and so everything went into chancery, with nobody the winner, the result was that the house was to be let to the Catholic Church and lived in by nun's.

A short time ahead of nuns moving in, a delegation came to stay with us. When asked to accompany them around the garden instead I conducted them down steps to an area through bramble patches and down deep dells, I was feeling cross as they had told me off for crossing my T's when I was trying to teach Adrian to write. They had reprimanded me! I had too much history from previous lives to take that on board.

After we had left Oakdown and before my grandparents were rehoused in the village. There was a time when the nuns let them stay on in the stables, in return for Nanny scrubbing the floors for them, how such a fiery lady, who fought for justice and was a friend and supporter of the suffragettes managed to do this I do not know. She was obviously a person of greater spirit than I realised. Towards the end of our life there, the bailiffs moved in, putting their coloured stickers on all the furniture. They stayed in the house and played games of cricket on the lawn with us. In total, they stayed for six weeks whilst the court case went on. The family came out of the situation penniless and with just small things in suitcases.

A new reality came into our lives. My brothers and sisters were placed into the care of various friends around the country, as neither of my parents had brothers or sisters. My grandparents were eventually rehoused in the village where Pop some time later fell from his window cleaning ladder hit his head and died, rather prematurely. Nanny was a widow for a very long time this was very sad as they had had a very happy and fulfilling marriage.

Simultaneously, while all this drama was going on, I became dangerously ill with Rheumatic fever. This was to leave me with a heart murmur for life.

I clearly remember the choice that was given as to whether my father or my grandfather was to carry me down the stairs to the waiting ambulance, on one side stood my grandmother wailing that you die in hospital. How cheerful was that for a child, so this was to be my rather ignominious lone exit from Oakdown. Transported to Hastings in an ambulance with a clanging bell, I was to be separated from my family for six months.

So there we are. This was to be the first time I was homeless. Moving home was to become rather familiar but at seven years old I was unable to remember who carried me down the stairs. Only now do I realise the pain it must have caused my mother to be parted from me when I was so ill and with her having to save what she could and to scatter the family around the country for some months.

There is a slight control thing in my life. It's important to know where I stand with people; my feet need to be on firm ground and not in a quicksand of indecision. Knowing exactly where I'm going makes me happy with anything as long as the major decisions in life are not taken out of my hands.

My finances, as well as my home, must be in my control so nothing like this will happen to me again. I have reached the stage when for the first time the decision rests with me concerning my life circumstances, my home and refuge.

I converted my current home from an old French remise — a barn — that was used for wine making which was a built of stone and standing on solid rock, with the great harsh hills of the Corbières around it. I can be anywhere in the world but knowing that its still here for me as my base rock my home and my eyrie to fly back to. This is the biggest luxury in life to know that it's my decision whether to stay or move and nobody else's.

The hospitalisation and unfortunate childhood situations helped to develop in me a stoicism that was to stand me in good stead for later life's upheavals, it enabled me to power on regardless of what life threw at me; just keep on walking as you never know what is around the corner, in retrospect perhaps I have been to strict with myself this time around, and must next learn the lesson of just falling back into the arms of trust and abandonment of all responsibility for my life, learn to just do it whatever it is, my guardians will look after me regardless. I even refused to drive a car until I understood how the engine worked. We all have something that we have to drop from our sack. Who knows, that way I might even learn to swim, if I could only trust the water. but perhaps abandonment of responsibilities was the last life and I just lay there having grapes peeled for me, This time I am over-adjusting, perhaps someone will turn up one day and knock my feet out from under me and then life can be really enjoyable, there again perhaps that's for next time.

Life was to be restricted, confined to bed in Hastings hospital flat on my back with no turning for the next six months. Although a few postcards came, I have no memories of any visits from my family at the time. They were scattered around the country deciding where to settle there was also a difficult post-war transport situation to contend with, remember it was not common to have a car at that time.

I was a very brave child who became a very brave adult and was the child who never cried the nurses all said what a good girl as there was never a tear. The thought of me as this little child makes me fill with anguish now, all emotions were squashed down for safety; my feeling was that if I cried it would be impossible for me to be able to stop. Only now do I know the damage that this did to me and allow tears to flow whenever they rise, far too embarrassingly often, as I have a problem stopping them. There is still a fear of separation even at my age, when new people arrive in my life; I keep trying to find out when they are planning to part and move on, so as just to get it over with, so strange.

The thought is ever-present and unnerving, I am still trying to sort that one and just enjoy the day and let everything pass on through whenever. We all have different hang-ups, however rich, gifted or beautiful we may be. It's just a matter of making the supreme effort to leave our hang-ups behind; now is the time to enjoy the moment as nothing else matters.

Whilst in hospital, and watching the other children with all their visitors, I have a clear memory of another child's mother giving me a ball made of silver paper wrapped around with a long piece of thin elastic. This made it possible for me when lying on my back in bed to throw the ball and have it return, that small breakout of freedom of movement is a powerful memory, I couldn't move but the ball could.

The long, lonely confinement possibly helped me to develop the natural ability of children to fly — to energetically leave the body— we all do it in our early youth. It was, at that time, the only way to remove myself from a difficult situation, it's something that I still do on occasion. When situations are getting stressful or when I absolutely want to visit a place or a friend and unable to get there I often just pop out on an astral visit. To be confined to bed for many months as a child, lying there with no physical activity, one develops a constant questing intelligence.

Everything came to an end a week before my ninth birthday, my grandparents turned up with a box of clothes. After them came mother and I was released from Hastings hospital to a whole new, painful and harsher world. Alas, the countryside was to vanish from my life for many years, only to be replaced by stone until my move to Suffolk, very many years later.

Mother turned up at the hospital one day, she had come to collect me with the news that we were to catch a train, and were to live in a house at Southsea; the rest of the family would follow soon. We walked down the hill from the Hospital to the station, as we did we were accompanied by the deafening sounds of chirping grasshoppers. Having been cut off from nature for so long I had forgotten what they were. I was still stunned by the dream unfolding before me, filled with amazement at the idea of living in Southsea a place that I was picturing as palm trees, hula skirts, coconuts and sandy beaches. It was going to be a childhood fantasy come true.

Well, Southsea was a bit of a comedown from my imaginary destination, it was Southsea in Portsmouth and not the South Seas that we were going to. We would be setting up home again, living in a rented house near the marine barracks at the wrong end of town. No sand just stones and the sewer outfall on the beach. My father then did a bizarre thing and opened a corner shop, this was very weird as he had a decidedly grand manner and was not in the habit of communicating with mere mortals, it was all a bit of a comedown from his grand start in life when he would shop with his mother in Harrod's. It was 1951 and my father stocked the corner shop with such odd things as tinned guavas and lychees. These, needless to say, soon turned up for pudding at home as the locals were rather mystified by such exoticism.

What was odd at this time, and I am at a loss to work it out, was that two of the maids from Oakdown and originally Brighton came with us. One worked in the shop and the other helped in the house with the children. They just appeared to follow us around for some years but who knows how they were paid. Mother was pregnant yet again with Celia this time, the last child of the family. So there we were, all together at the seaside again, just a few roads back from the seafront where we spent our playtime mucking about at the edge of the water.

This being early in the nineteen fifty such things as sewage outfalls were not as sanitary as they should be. So I promptly caught Polio from the effluent in the sea, this was in what turned out to be the last epidemic of that illness in England. I distinctly remember the floppy helplessness but I was only ill for a few weeks. However the effects are with me for life as my left side is shorter than my right with some muscles missing from under the left shoulder blade, could be worse.

The last decade of my life plus any spare money, has been devoted too repairing the damage from this and a series of back accidents, all is with help from a Chiropractor, Deep massage and Acupuncture. I have a long time to last out yet, and I can't stand anything stopping me doing just what I want with my body or — *my vehicle*—as my guides call it. I hope that my body will last out in good condition as there is just too much to discover and do in my general overall plan for the next twenty years, or so.

Chapter Ten

*If you judge a fish by its ability to climb a tree,
it will live its whole life believing its stupid*

Albert Einstein

So here I am, still here still very fit, and with the help of my guides plenty of work ahead for me to do, in fact as much as I wish to take on.

The one thing that life has taught me is that however dark the road is you never know what is going to turn up around the next corner. On occasions, it has taken my breath away in astonishment. When I look back on the route my life has taken, it is a constant revelation to me to regard the serendipitous pattern left behind in the sand of my life. All the byways that I often tottered along, that appeared meaningless at the time, are later revealed in retrospect.

We moved house in Southsea and Portsmouth quite a lot, it was always — here we go yet again- new local schools — many — and again being laughed at, now for my Sussex accent and not my Nottingham one — back to teasing and calls of "Oy! ginger". I learnt at an early age to be confident with myself and walk my life alone, not seeking to follow anybody, I'm still am not a follower and am perhaps a rather self-willed impatient, horse without a saddle or bridle that would be good description of me. I find it is preferable to have my friends and animals to be rather the same, independent minded and never a fawning spaniel or Labrador as adoring obedience irritates me.

Remember two things about life: first, always know where you are going; secondly, know who is going with you —never the other way around or you will land up off your soul's chosen path.

We are in this world to experience and develop, and that's more powerful when one is in this dimension that is denser and darker. We do all collaborate and choose the task's and experience's we wish to pursue, when here, everything is a development of what we were only able to imagine before we arrived.

As a family we hung together moving, from pillar to post and wherever our mother found a suitable house to rent. One day we moved house whilst we were at school, we were collected and taken to another place at home time, this possibly might have been done to not disturb us with the apprehension of an upcoming change but in fact it did the opposite and has left me with an inclination to want to know everything that is going on concerning my life and who everyone is in relation to my life, and what it involves. This insecure package from childhood is something that I am working on; I live with trust that the safety net will always be there for me and my guides will protect me, and guard my back. I am constantly amazed at the love and care that I receive from them if I just trust. Hopefully it will be sorted when the time comes to move on to whatever may come next in this life, or the next.

So the final area for growing up was in Hampshire, attending various schools, none of which were able to understand or have the time to sort out whatever was the problem with my brain. I could read avidly, there was nothing printed that was not worth reading even the cereal packet. I had read many of the Shakespeare plays by the age of fourteen, but was still unable to construct a sentence without writing both words and sentences back to front and the clock I still read backwards.

Into my life came a friend who understands my brain and how it works, she has studied dyslexia, written a book on the subject, and has travelled to the Far East teaching teachers and students the system and workings of the dyslexic brain.

She understands how we are often more intelligent and have rapid systems of comprehension and unlike the so called standard brain, we are free-range. It's rather like an open-plan house with no barriers, we just see and jump to the answer as we open the front door. Often we are very physical and kinaesthetic in how we learn, this was a revelation to me, having always been cast aside and written off by teachers as rather dim although my IQ score was high. Happy this problem in education is now being addressed, and no longer is any child written off.

Chapter Eleven

No one can make you feel inferior without your consent.

Eleanor Roosevelt

WE were six children now, the last one being Celia. Father continued with the shop, but his failure as a shop keeper was always going to be inevitable as it was an unsuitable trade for him, nothing could have been so remote from my father. He was not a very social person and had a style of communication which was always vague and distant I realise that he was what is referred to as borderline autistic.

As a child, my father would open the door to me at tea-time he would look at me and say "Oh, it's you" as if at four o'clock it would be anybody else, and like all children in large family we were often given whatever name came to mind first.

After giving up the shop we were in the usual calamitous situation regarding money and a home. All this meant that my parents decided that they needed to train as publicans as that way there would always be a roof over our heads and the heating bill paid for. The only problem with this idea was how to retrain when you had six children in tow.

Oh dear, that conclusion was very ominous, we were to arrive at our final destination in a roundabout way, and as usual, were riding very close to the cliff edge, one might say.

A plan was devised for Julian to go into temporary care in Hayling Island; Adrian went to live with his old Nurse who appeared to be looking after him for love not money. Celia being a tot stayed and moved to London with our parents whilst they did their training. All this was to leave Geraldine Isabel and me. Gerry, the brightest and a scholarship girl, decided to go to London to train and work as a cook, she wanted to get out into the world and earn money. She has passed on now and her life story was a poignant one.

My mother did something next, that has amazed many of my friends since. But understand that things were dire, she had to find a way of keeping a roof over our heads and food for the family my father was just not reliable as a provider. She placed an advert in the window of the greengrocers shop asking for a good home for two teenage girls for six months. This was to be whilst they went to London and retrained to be publicans. It made Isabel and me sound like a couple of homeless dogs.

Isabel was an apprentice hairdresser at the time and stayed with me, we were safe and housed with our temporary family. So I continued my system of shutting down and keeping a low profile. It was not too hard for me as so far I'd had plenty of practice. In retrospect, what my mother did to get us a home was not such an outrageous act, in England at that time it was quite the norm for children to be sent away from home to live at boarding school, in what turns out often to be very rough circumstances surrounded by hordes of semi savage children, and potential paedophiles. We at least did have each other and two responsible adults in a house with us. Whilst Bell was out at work or out with her boyfriends I ended-up having to do rather a lot of the housework for the family where we stayed, when I was not called to run out to the shop for cigarettes for our substitute mother, I was a bit of a household skivvy — Cinderella. They were kind enough but had two children already and we were just there for the extra income.

Here we go again — yet another move — the eighth, I think, so far all involving new schools. I had, by now, developed the skill of just fading into the background, anything for a quiet life, also at this time, with the post-war baby boom; it was the norm to have a class of forty-five students as a minimum. I've genuinely lost count of all the schools that I have attended or the houses that my childhood was lived in. They have just vanished into a blur, they are unimportant.

Six months later, life was looking up and we all moved into a pub on the Gosport quay-side of Portsmouth harbour. It was at this stage of my life that I learnt how to negotiate a passage through drunken submariners or any other rough scenes; it was to become the skill which would serve me well in the many of the difficult parts of London that I was to live in later.

Never be fearful, fear can be smelt a mile off, wear shoes you can run in and never be or feel a victim, always be confident that you are a giant, and are surrounded by your helpers, think of them as motorcycle outriders, with all their love and protection they are always with you. To that end I learnt how to take command of my own life, being very grown up for my age and not used to having a father who was overprotective, remember he never enquired where I had been or who my friends were, but he gave me all the intellectual stimulation that was needed, he had a very good brain. We were able to discuss everything philosophical and artistic.

Once I was out sight, I was running pretty near the wind at times; it was all a case of what the parents didn't see would not worry them. Just as long as I appear at ten thirty, closing time in not too much of a disarray and ready to help with the glass washing and bottling-up then all was OK.

At home my parents encouraged me in the direction of the Arts. So when school was coming to an end, and the teachers suggested that I should go to the local factory as a machinist, I was amazed at such a thought and demanded to go to the local Art College in Portsmouth.

The next stage was to attend a special fourth-form school for late developers and students who had missed out on the system for one reason or another and had never taken an exam. This turned out to be a very good time in my life as, for the first time, I was surrounded by people who were all oddballs; it felt like home not school and for me was so comfortable. We had just two teachers and they were the first same sex couple that I remember being in contact with, one was tall and thin and wore a tweed skirt and a twin-set with a glass bead necklace, she was devoted to the Pre-Raphaelites and taught us Art, History and Literature, Greek and Roman mythology and all the other not so very useful but wonderful add-ons to an education.

The other teacher was rather short and fat, she also wore a tweed skirt and a painter's smock; she taught us art pottery and drawing.

These figures were to be a future inspiration for Grace and Flo, the names that I give to two of my guardian angels who were to appear so much more powerfully in my life at a later date. I did not realise until much later on that one's guides and helpers use the information that you have, to work with and through you to achieve what they and you would wish to achieve, if they look familiar they will not frighten you at the start of your relationship, but the image fades with time, and they revert to powerful energies.

When I finished school and Managed to get to Art college it was a big relief as at that time it was possible to receive assistance that enabled students from large families to attend, so in due time a transport pass arrived for me. This was a great advantage as living on the wrong side of Portsmouth Harbour I needed to commute by boat. The novelty of catching the ferry to college each day was in itself a delight except in snow. There were many times in the early morning when the mouth of the harbour was crossed by a school of dolphins, plus when coming home at night in the dark with just the boat lights and the smell and sound of dark water, that will be always with me, that sound is from my race memory, the Dutch side of me.

My love and affinity with the sea causes me to suffer serious withdrawal effects. I just need to sit and stare at the sea. One of my favourite memories since living on the European mainland was of taking the boat to England from Rotterdam. Five hours staring at a cold, grey sea soothes many deeply hidden things. Genetically I am very much from the water. After all my genes are from Friesland as well as England.

It was only in recent years that I realised the importance of balance in one's childhood and achieving a complete understanding as to where one comes from. This helps to ground and centre us as we link in with our DNA as well as enabling us to perform the clearing work with our ancestors, it helps us to develop from a firm base.

It was unfortunate for us children, although we had two sets of grandparents that were still alive, my Dutch grandparents, though living in England, refused to acknowledge us. I was a child at the time and I assumed that this was a normal occurrence. My father's parents refused to interact with us even though he was their only child and they had gained six grandchildren. I saw them only once when very young, when we were taken to visit but were completely rejected. I realise now that this was due to their extreme religious belief's, so that was the last time I saw them. My mother was deemed a "scarlet woman" as she was a singer and on the stage. The fact that she sang in opera and at concerts, made no difference. After a revelatory short trip to Amsterdam in recent years, I now realise the effect of unbalance that this rejection had caused me at a deep level.

Staying for a few days on a boat moored on the Amstel was wonderful. I was completely mesmerised by the surroundings and the boats, I was almost in a trance as the water lapped at the base of the window. Some boats that were near to me were Boomschuits; the type of boat that was used by the family for many centuries, hence my surname name van der Schuit.

It is important to realise how we carry a genetic memory as well as a past life memory. We are but a melting pot of all our experiences in all dimensions. By coincidence, or not, at the same time, there was someone who had started to research my family history online. They had discovered family records on the Friesian side back to the fifteenth century.

These experiences gave me deep healing and understanding. It had filled in my missing parts, counteracting the lopsided feeling I had. Often I think that the family rejection from one side and the many casual rejections and cut-offs from love in my life have gone on to manifest my lopsided body and wobbly heart. We physically take on — manifest — the emotional hurts we receive in life, I can now rise above all, as it made me who I am and I chose it.

On this front I thought all was well and sorted, but no, as many years later it still gave me a twinge when asking a friend about her upbringing it came out that when as a student she had a cleaning job in the house next to my Dutch grandparents house, the house that my father had designed and furnished for them in his early days as a draughtsman. She knew more of their home than I ever did. That hurt, but take it on understand and progress.

Chapter Twelve

> Its no good going back to yesterday because
> I was a different person then.
>
> Lewis Carol

OFF to college, it was to be a time of great learning, diving in and doing classes in anything that was available day or night. Then, as now, learning new things has become compulsive and still I am unable to get enough knowledge. There is always something new and surprising to find out around the next corner. Every course at college that I enrolled on has been used later in life to earn a living hence the gilt framed — Ancora Imparo - hanging on the wall above my desk.

At that time, although surrounded by boys and casual encounters, I found most of them were just too boring. There was nothing there between the ears, just an uninquiring void. I was set in this world needing intellect as much as a sexual encounter. I'm hard pushed to remember any individual male encounters, until bang, unexpectedly whilst having a night out at a college "Hop" just before my seventeenth birthday, when dressed up as a goldfish or something bizarre, when on returning inside to the dance, having just escaped from the rather over amorous clutches of an arrogant architect in the car park, I was resting against a pillar for a minute when a young man not known to me, did the classic mate's trick he came up to me and said "My friend back there wants to talk to you". As I turned around I saw John, and instantly thought "Oh there you are". It was as if he had just been out of the room for just a few minutes. I knew who he was and that we were back again for another turn at this living thing and I knew him so well from many times before. We have often been together, you always recognise old close companions from the other side and other lives.

John started a conversation with me concerning Viridian coloured bridges in Nairobi and we never stopped laughing and talking about everything under the sun for the next fifty years. Always intuitively knowing that I was one of the favoured ones who was incarnated with their soul mate, this was later confirmed by my guides — our soul mate is the spirit that we spend most of our time with on the other side, it's a wonderful way of spending one's life but it also has its downsides.

He was my closest friend, my teacher, my lover, my reason for being here. I desperately missed all of those sides of him, and still do — no you don't grow out of it. When long term partners part and go from here, it takes a bit of time to adjust to the strange world of other male energies that come into the vacuum. It's a process many others go through many times in a single lifetime, but after hitting the target the first time, its leaves one shocked and ignorant of the rules of play when one is only used to total trust and unconditional love.

There is a big difference between falling head over heels in love, which is hormonal, very enjoyable and can be fallen out of rapidly. But unreservedly loving and combining with a person, on all levels the spiritual, as well the physical, i.e. sexual. This is not a thing that you can fall out of, it is a desire to always be with a person regardless of the circumstances' life brings, never to doubt them, never desire to change them, totally trust them and care for them whatever turns up.

When it's over, the best way is to walk forward and be content that you had a good time. Not every life we've lived was like that, we all have bad ones as well as good ones. If another like-minded individual turns up on your path and is going in the same direction and if they are in alignment, that's going to be a bonus but don't bet on it. Just stay open to whatever turns up. Never close the doors as who knows what delights might turn up in the final stages. Always wait for the fat lady to sing.

So there we go, first base on the journey of a long life, when you meet up with your soul-mate and close friend from the other side they are so familiar one hardly waits for an introduction. There is no shyness or getting to know old friends, one just takes up with the conversation from before you last separated. On the other side, one lives in close groups in one's larger soul family. My subgroup had just three members, later in life after John's passing; I went on to meet up with the third member who was a much younger spiritually. That encounter, although very confusing, helped me to remember never to be embarrass and hide who I am, the only important thing is to be totally open and honest on all counts to avoid confusion, never allow oneself to become distorted and to hide ones true self from another.

We all take on different roles: we are here to just experience things, to enact things, and to develop which is why it is intended that we loose the memory of our real place and our spiritual home. If we were to be conscious of all past lives, the experience here would not be so meaningful. There are times when we might wish to understand and know what the experience is to enact a real unloving indifference, cruelty or hate. The one thing I find hardest to understand is how another soul might wish to experience suffering this time around. But I do understand the value of how getting out of bed to go to work for one person, can be the equivalent of another climbing Everest. All need to be admired for their individual effort, not judged one against another. Try to always suspend judgement, that's extraordinarily hard to do when a human.

I am still in touch with memories from some of my other lives and death's, as I'm a bit *leaky*. It can be a bit of a burden to carry with you, as that's where many of our ungrounded fears originate; they resonate onwards from past lives. In most of my previous lives I have been with plants and herbs as a healer. I have been an Elemental — a plant guardian — a Shaman, Witch, and a Wise woman. Among my many visits to this dimension I have covered most of these labels; all derive from my place of origin that was of nature and healing. We all are from, and return to, various training places and learning groups when we are between lives.

It has not been comfortable for me a lot of the time as I have lived many of my lives in great hardship, alone and in complete isolation, far from society, ostracised, feared and treated with derision and usually killed rather nastily because of people's fear of me, this I still pick up around people sometimes often there is a sense of guardedness, about them when in my company.

Living outside of society in poverty, deep in forests and not always following a straight path in life, there have been times when I have by using my skills and have been a manipulator of things and people, not for bad results I hope.

Although in this life, I appear to be very social, and at the centre of things, I am still very much a loner and conscious of my choice of friends. I am adamant in only having a loose link in connection to others in my life now, everyone must be free. In another life I had arranged to put an enticement on someone, that's so bad to interfere with another. Also for instance, ten lives ago, there were four husbands and vows were made to love each one forever. Well, that would be impossible as forever is forever and they would never be free of me, or I of them. That had to be rectified in this dimension. I was also guilty of enticing a soul facet from another and still had it with me in this life, although it was given to me freely, it had to be sorted out and returned to him in this dimension, This was to enable me to clear the shadowy debris left from previous incarnations, as it all hampers progress.

Probably the latter is the reason why in this lifetime there are so many men that I have met up with, that are often from former lives. They appear in my current life, many needing a time of help and repair before they pass on their way. The damage was not inflicted by me but it is my job to just make an energetic space for them to repair. They appear so regularly and have done so as long as I remember. Two that were helped by me have now long passed across. I was just touching base and putting things right before they passed. It never bothered John, without discussing the matter he just accepted it, we rarely discussed anything of profound significance to do with who I am, he just instinctively knew and accepted. In fact, he brought life battered people home to me and asked if I could help them as if they were stray cats. I always think he was spiritually older than me and subliminally knew a lot about me that I was unaware of, he was here with me to keep me safe.

Never take a hold over another is my prime rule in this existence. Let others be and never manipulate. Just stand back and help when asked. The latter is very hard to do as my inclination is to rush in and help. I can't stand broken things, even furniture and china in my life, and all things and people that wish to be restored are restored.

We need to learn when to let people live the route that they planned however disastrous it might be, think before leaping to the rescue, don't disempower. It's not easy but we are never in a position to judge anybody as we have almost certainly been there as well at some time and we have probably forgotten the experience. We have no superiority over others in this or any other life. Before we come to this vibrational level on planet earth, we undertake sessions of meticulous planning with significant others who will play an important role in our future life. General outlines are planned ahead but the whole thing of living here is that we are with our guides and always with our personal carers, many people refer to these as their guardian angels, perhaps they are our towering guardian outriders? We only have to ask for help and it will be there.

We do have free will and we do not have to follow our soul's desire. Our soul "or spirit" sends us on its mission but its up to us here in this dimension with ego on a trip with us to decide whether we wish to carry it through to the end. We have limitless lives, but we do know when we are on the right route because that's the time when we experience an overwhelming passion for what we are doing, pure joy and bliss we fly along with a sense of purpose. All things turn to our advantage and slip into place effortlessly as we discover the constant serendipity of life, things and people you need at the time without knowing it, just turn up mysteriously, this is because you have picked up the connecting cord with your soul's desire and that is when you see the opportunities and fearlessly leap to them, they were always there but we were ignoring them. We were often blind to the obvious.

When lost in the midst of life's confusion, not knowing where to turn and which road to take at the crossroad, try to be still and cast the ego aside, and try to forget the need for money — that's not easy. Then think of what your passion is and follow its trail. Passion is the one true guide that can be relied on. It's not easy as the ego interferes constantly trying to steer our life in its own desired direction. Its role is very important but it's only of this earth and it does not belong to us on any other level, just the body.

On the higher spiritual level we are at one with the source of all things and we definitely don't need an ego there. Ego gets in the way when we allow it to dominate as it's too logical and acts like a terrier at the door, protecting us, it can be the source of all trouble, ills and arguments, small and universal. When you feel that you are deeply hurt move the ego aside and communicate from the soul. It's amazing how easy it is, you can't be hurt on a soul level only on an ego one. There is an overwhelming feeling of freedom when placing ego to one side.

Listen to the gut feeling, it's your guides prompting you, it's the only real feeling of soul communication that will align you with both your own and your soul's intentions and desires. The true, very quiet answer will vibrate through the body, the reason that we are here on this earth is the development of our soul. The constant feeling of low level unhappiness that never really leaves us, derives from our separation from source, we are only separated in our mind as this vibration level is much denser.

This life is a short interlude, a dream, on return to source, we are at one in our true dimension, we imagined this dimension into reality, the world and we as an individual person are just figments of our souls devising, both world and body are a sea of vibrating atoms nothing is solid they are the vehicle for our soul to experience its desire, and aid its development. Unlike what many people might tell you, this not a place of punishment or a school of hard learning, address every situation with unconditional love, suspend your constant judgement — judgement is fear — then love will reflect back to you from everything and everybody that you come in contact with.

Chapter Thirteen

We are all broken that's how the light gets in.
Earnest Hemingway

As I was saying earlier, this was to be the start of a long and interesting soul-mate relationship with John; it lasted for fifty years starting from just before my seventeenth birthday. In no way was our relationship always easy, in fact for me it was to be a time of learning how to put down deep roots, and grow tall in my own space, without any other person overshadowing me.

Being married to a much older person and a Scorpio, a very old and wise soul with all the charisma attached, I quickly had to learn how to stand tall. To be here with a soul-mate is a joy. Never was there a glimmer of jealousy or distrust between us. John worked surrounded by women, and I worked almost exclusively with males, and although brought up in a family that was predominately female, I was always very comfortable with men, feeling that the egos they hide behind are so large and fragile. Men live under such pressure from society. to be male, to look after everyone, never to be vulnerable, to be a good provider, and to be brilliant sexually etc., etc., the whole rucksack of junk, that is dumped on their small shoulders as little boys is so heavy.

All of us look back at some time and say I shouldn't have done that or should have done this. Making mutually loving and developing relationships is the hardest thing we have to do. It's a job in itself. Mine was a relationship of great love and insights, an enormous amount of love and respect flowed between us and still does. But in retrospect I should have spoken up for what I wanted as well. Perhaps a few more holidays instead of restoring house projects might have been in order.

Being guilty of doing a silly thing early on in our marriage has always bugged me. It became my habit to step back for many years. We were both artists at the start of our relationship, until one day a South African doctor friend, who was a collector of young artists works, saw some of my paintings; thought that they were John's and commented on how much he liked them. I did a very strange thing then I stopped painting, I did not want to detract from John's work. When John passed, his studio became mine. I then returned to my first love of painting my emotions. In retrospect, being so compliant was not needed but I was always stepping back, always suppressing feelings or tears that might upset the constant desire to make others happy.

John was very English in his way of expressing himself. Some time after he passed, I was staying with a dear mutual friend whose husband had recently died. We were reminiscing when she said that on asking John one day, did he love me from the start, he replied that he adored me from the first day and every day since. That hit me in the solar plexus so hard. What was so painfully sad was that he could say that to my friend and never to me, but there we are that's life with an Englishman.

The words don't need to be said out loud; but it's lovely if they are, love expressed in this dimension is so supportive and nurturing. It's only a word but one that my life was very short of, it helps people to grow its like water is for a plant it helps one expand. In my memory my mother only said she loved me once after childhood. It was when I was not much older than a child and vastly pregnant. I was saying goodbye to her on Waterloo station at the time. My father never said he loved me. He was always very distant with a rather Edwardian manner, but life was different then, very different. It was not a common thing for the English to express their feelings in words, it might have been a left over from the war with its constant stiff upper lip - and don't be soppy.

A few years after John had passed and I had moved into my new home I had a very moving experience. A new friend came into my life she had made a place essence. These are a vibrational essence made in a significant place. The essence was made high-up on land that I was to come to know so well later. When she had sat down to make the essence, unbeknown to me a newly hatched yellow butterfly had sat on the rim of the bottle opened its wing's and then flew up into the sky. This was not told to me until some time later. When she gave the essence to me she just said here you are I think I've made this for you.

So, sitting with the opened bottle I was almost immediately whisked away into what appeared to be a very blue sea or very blue sky surrounded by bright yellow. The feeling was of overwhelming freedom, joy, and expansion it was just "Wow" for me as at that time as I was in a very grey place of grief.

On surfacing and coming back into my self, I took immediate action and removed the photo of John from the frame and threw the frame away. It was a dreadful act to have captured him in that prison of a photo frame. The photo had been taken the year before his death and at the time that he was so dreadfully ill. Photo frames capture people and imprison them.

After the experience with the place essence, I drove to the jewellers for my wedding ring to be cut off, and then altered to fit my right hand. On arriving back home after doing this I had an overwhelming feeling of exuberant elation, it was not just me experiencing it, the feeling in the house was ebullient, it was full of overwhelming gratitude. I was surrounded by joy, it was as though I had let John free, and loosened the ties between us.

He was no longer tied to the Earth and me. A while later when thoroughly on my own two feet, the ring was removed all together. A wedding ring symbolised a promise of fidelity in marriage and we are both released from that promise now. There is no point in making marriage vows or even being married if you do not honour them in thought and action. One can't restrain or hold onto another being in this dimension or any other. For our soul's development we all need freedom.

Well, John is still around me and not just when I need his help, when he is near a sudden rush of tears come. This was hard at the start as I was not expecting a visit. He often pops in to check things out and do a bit of manoeuvring. There is always a knowing when it's him that's been fixing things behind the scenes. Sometimes, when things are getting a bit tight financially, unexpected money appears from an unexpected source. On passing a shop or stall something stands out and hits me in the eye and I know that John would have urged me to buy it and I would love it. So the time has come to learn how to spoil my self and get myself a small thing that he would have purchased either on my birthday or Christmas, it's all a matter of the ongoing project many of us have, learning to love ourselves.

Getting back again to where we were. Returning to the time after Art College had finished, I moved to London to start work in the buying department of Jaeger. John had arrived just before me so we were together again and after my spending a short spell in the YWCA opposite the British Museum, we moved into two rooms at the top of a house in Muswell Hill. The year was 1960 and contraception was still unreliable with the inevitable result. I became pregnant and gave birth to a baby girl.

This was how we started our married life as many others did at that time in a two room basement flat in Camden Town with a baby girl. This was a difficult time in my life a time of great loneliness, hunger and poverty. John was taking a teaching certificate to add to his degree as our life had changed with the start of a family. He was not supposed to be married as rules were strict then and money was very short. I was so desperate to contribute and did a silly thing, ten days after having the baby. I tried to work, in the evening, so after John's return home I went to Lyons corner house scrubbing milk boilers out. That was a failure as I was very anaemic exhausted and undernourished so gave it up.

Food was meat, fish or eggs on Friday, with porridge and vegetables picked up after the market closed on other days. I am a high protein, vegetables and fruit eater and need a lot of minerals from nuts and seeds. Carbs, as in bread and pasta, just kill and depress me. In fact bread makes me feel in deep black hole of depression. Give us our daily bread sounds horrifying to me. I had no idea how to feed us with so little money, and becoming weak and extremely thin, I was unable to feed the baby because of abscesses' on my breasts arms and legs. At that time there was no real help from the State, just free orange juice and dried milk for the baby. I told no one of our situation as I did not want the baby taken away. We managed with an income of ten pounds a week, the rent being five pounds from the other five pounds and we had to pay all service outgoings and food.

All was not lost, as a little later a job with a couturier fashion house on the other side of Regents Park came up, so I walked through the park to work. It was easy to pick up dumped returnable bottles on the way back from work; this enabled me to collect the deposits that were then used to buy food for supper before going home.

Although there was no obligation placed on me, I had a need to work as the responsibility for the baby's birth was mine as well as John's and I wished to contribute towards the family income as well. Our daughter went daily to be cared for by a wonderful Greek lady who adored her. This enabled me to stay in my job for about a year. It was not a comfortable job for me, as it involved rather a lot of bobbing and scraping to members of the aristocracy and I am not very good at the "Yes, my Ladyship" role as I come from a decidedly feminist and socialist background.

Chapter Fourteen

> Stay away from negative people they
> have a problem for every solution
>
> Albert Einstein

LIKE many others of my generation, there is a clear remembrance of the effect that The Cuba Missile Crisis had on us. Many since have underplayed it but we who were there just knew its significance. The news of it just hit the pit of the stomach. After returning home one evening I was making dinner and heard the news of the stand-off between Russia and America. I turned off the cooking and went to the American embassy to protest, as I considered that to be very important.

This is a remarkable thing was done by an enormous amount of Londoners and to this day I still have the feeling that the outrageous confrontation was a pivotal moment in world safety, and am glad that I contributed my commitment to peace.

All my life I have been on many protests signed and set up many petitions. Since the days of Cuba and Rachel Carson's book "*Silent Spring*," life has changed radically and now it's a whole new scenario. Whilst we were all occupied with shopping and nesting, we let the power slip unnoticed into different hands.

I have become more than a little cynical now, and realise that a few thousand people killed here or there means absolutely nothing to those in charge. It's just something to distract us from noticing what is really going on behind the scenes. We have been turned into beings with a short attention span that only become animated by disasters and dramas, as they pull at our strings. The more energy we put into reacting to them, the more we are distracted from the real undercover interconnectedness of the worlds monetary and government scenario.

We react like a herd of terrified sheep, rushing this way and that at the behest of the newspaper correspondents. When we fear a situation, we provide it with the fuel to grow into a monster, withdraw your energy from what those few in charge are trying to frighten you with. Put it to good use doing something positive to help the world in your individual, small life. Hold a space of enlightenment — that means bringing the light down, positively, to this dimension.

If, and only when we all do that will we start to make progress, into a world of adult give and take discussion, and not childish irresponsible, violence and war.

> *The strange thing is that we forget how powerful one person is. Each person individually makes up the sum total of the whole world. Never think that it's too much for one to take on. We are that entire one. If each one of us should be concerned about our own input and not constantly running about discussing and magnifying fears, adding fuel the general hysteria. We can turn each small negative into a positive. Negative thoughts make a negative reality. Our thoughts are more powerful than we could ever realise. They can move the world.*
>
> *Our thought's manifest both ours and the worlds' reality, when in our human state, we have no conception of the giants that we really are, and how dare (whoever and whatever it might be) try to frighten us? Each one of us is a co-creator of this world.*

The media and newspapers earn their living by generating a constant drama drip feed, and we are addicted to it. Just take a quick look at the news, check it out on the computer, open a newspaper and our addiction is fed for a few more hours. The longer we stay in this state of mind, we are powerless. We live by drama, the TV and radio are full of it every day — it's an addiction. When there is something horrid in the wardrobe don't panic, step forward and open the door.

We are fed on a diet of fear and secrecy to overwhelm us, if we are swayed by it, we will allow others to steal our power, and hold us back, from our role as the elevated beings of light, that we all have the potential to become. Grow, step forward from the herd of sheep become the energy giant that you have the blueprint potential to be. Never, Never, Never, give your power away.

Only when we realise that this place that we exist in is just a figment of our imagination, just a dream space that we have put ourselves in, all that it is and ever will be is just a dream interlude. Realise that we are a small part of the greater source, experiencing the dream. It is a very beautiful dream at times and a nightmare at others, but it's only a dream. When we return to Source, only then will we see how very small and insignificant we have allowed ourselves to become.

We have not been rejected — thrown out of the garden of Eden — we turned our back on it and became fragmented from the only true Source, our ego has told us that we are each different, but when we turn back to Source the ego is redundant.

After the hard times of Camden town we had a stroke of luck, it came via some old college friends who had decided to move to the country. So they passed their rented basement flat in Notting Hill on to us, the flat was the normal type of basement flat, comprising two large rooms that were the old kitchens, with a courtyard out front, because it were on a hill, we had a lower floor to the garden at the back. This lower floor in time John turned into a study for him, and next to it, a sewing room for me. Out the back was a shared private three acre iron fenced garden overlooked by the two vast blocks of Victorian four storey houses. All of this was wonderful luck as I was now expecting my second child a boy.

We were very happy in Notting Hill; it was a colourful multi-cultural area and had the famous Portobello market just around the corner, a wonderful place for food and bargain hunting and we lived in the flat for many years, making friends who have stayed with us for a lifetime. We formed a mutual child support system, that way we all helped each other to work by looking after each other's children. Either having two children with us or no children, and the children always had companions. It was a good system if your child fell down they understood there were others to pick them up when needed.

At this time my neighbour was making costumes at home for theatres and advertising. As sewing was my major skill and I had just had my twenty-first birthday, I was able to buy a sewing machine on hire-purchase, joining my neighbour sewing during school hours. At last this was the start of earning a reasonable supplement to the household income without leaving the house. Before long, I went on to alter couture clothes for duchesses and make costumes for strippers, whatever came my way, even running a theatre wardrobe.

John was moving through the system of Polytechnic and University teaching, even though the income was unexciting, it was steady, and he had long times off for his many projects. One of these being a birthday surprise of a full size copy of one of the artist Ben Nicholson's white reliefs. I still have it hanging on my sitting room wall. He was always full of magical surprises. He just adored creating beautiful things.

The sixties were a time of great creative energy. They were in full swing with plenty of work about, everyone worked and played around the clock. I alternated between sewing for theatre costumers and working for the rag trade making things for the small Carnaby Street shops or for the well off; the latter being very hard to work for at times, I had to suspend my belief that "I am the queen of Portugal" as I am not very good at suffering rich fools gladly.

Work was always there if one had a sewing machine and a creative bent. I have never lacked confidence in knowing what I can do and this has enabled me to often step into jobs that other's might have baulked at, I just grab the chance and say yes.

London in the sixties was the centre of the world of fashion, so I was often called to the big hotels to take up skirt hems and run through wardrobes for overseas visitors, bringing the clothes up to date and advising them on what to wear for what and when.

At the same time, as all this was going on there was an influx of draft dodgers from America. The area was awash with them and they lay head to toe down the corridors of our flats and houses in the area. Notting hill was humming. No one had much money and we were all used to living in cramped flats, but our doors were always open as we helped each other and shared food when things were tight and when paid we celebrated.

This was really life as we made it and how it would be nice to always live. We had really sound friends and lots of shared suppers. Friends are the people who you can call at three in the morning for help when there is a disaster. They in turn can be confident that they can do the same. Life is really too short and too intense for any other type of friend. As one moves around, there is always a new friend to add or another drifts away, but the nucleus stays.

Having and keeping friends is a female thing. They have the social skills it takes to work at keeping all the plates spinning, possibly caring for children and making contact with other mothers set up the habit. Men are really loners. They have a system of super concentration and rely on women as a rule for social contacts.

Life was not always good for me at that time. In Notting hill my life was cut off from the natural world of gardening. The patch of land at the back of the flat was rock hard and dry it was overshadowed by a giant plane tree so no gardening for me, just pots in the front courtyard. It was later I found out how bad it is for me to live in this situation. It is crucial for me to touch base with the earth each day to do some planting or weeding or perhaps just sitting and being with the plants whilst having a cup of tea at an early hour or wandering around for a chat with them, from time to time in the day.

The problem of alienation from nature and being ungrounded came to a head one day, I was about to go out on a sewing job, when I found myself unable to pass through the front door as each time when I stepped outside, I was shaking and feeling as if I was about to fly off the world, It was as if gravity was no longer working. The season was summer and for a time I wore a heavy coat and Wellington boots to keep grounded as I was so nervous.

The area was swamped with drugs at that time, and I was constantly surrounded by people with scrambled vibrations, anything like that just seeps through and is disastrous for me. I knew nothing about protecting myself at that time. I have had to learn everything the long hard way, we had no advice handbooks and no internet — it was a very different world. Friends helped with the children and John was patient as much as his work allowed, he took me for out for a walk in the evenings, but these walks were so painful, with me holding onto the railings to stop the tendency to float off. I became so sensitised to everything I was feeling like a radio receiver, picking up every feeling and thought of those around me and the outside world, there was no off switch. It was a form of torture. I now know the answer to this all too well; I need to lie down on the ground at least three times a day to thoroughly ground myself.

In later life when working as a healer, I found that this was important for many of my patients, the ones that lived off the ground in flats wearing nylon socks, rubber soled shoes and artificial carpets, just standing on the ground outside without socks and shoes for a short time each day helped calm the nervous system, and if done last thing at night it is good for promoting sleep.

The main problem with my being ungrounded is that I am super sensitive and have such porous peripheries. There is very little in the way of a barrier and this causes me to take up other's negative energy. Often when looking at people I see they are full of shadows, the residue of so much negativity. Unless I remember to be protected, it hits me and crashes into my heart centre, It has taken me another fifty years to partially rectify this problem, If only I had realised or been given the information at that time a great deal of heartache and damage to my health might have been avoided.

My friends looked at me as a problem to be sorted, so helpfully they trotted me along to the doctor and being me, I foolishly told him about my feelings and the fact that I was surrounded by people who were not there in this dimension. What a silly thing to tell a doctor. He dosed me up with appalling and now long banned mind controlling drugs for suppressing and livening up around the clock each day. Within the first twenty-four hours of the mind bending drugs they had a dreadful impact on me, I had a strong desire to kill myself on returning to the doctor he said, ah yes they have this effect some people. Great, how helpful! He then gave me something even worst that rapidly turned me into a zombie — safe, able to feed my children and not to be too much of an inconvenience to society.

I am extremely sensitive to all drugs and this too was a dreadful thing to happen to me. In time, I was sent as an out patient to the Maudsley mental hospital, then one wonderful day a new psychiatrist asked me "Do you drink coffee"? "Oh yes", I said, "about five or six cups a day." That's it! It was like magic. At last, an intelligent doctor with an enquiring mind, who actually looked at what I ate or drank! Coffee is like poison to me and it's been impossible for me to drink Gunpowder or Earl Grey tea either, I can't have stimulants of any sort or I take off from the planet or land up with heart palpitations. At least I can drink alcohol — OK! In fact, I have checked it out with *The Management,* alcohol is approved of in moderation—a decent glass of red in the evening is definitely allowed.

Coffee was stopped, the drugs were thrown away, but still there was a constant illusion of walking along a very high and very narrow wall, over the months this slowly sank to the ground the path began to broaden, and I was able to leave the house, I found a temporary job in the sales in Oxford Street.

Travelling on the tube and being in the crowds was a kill or cure treatment. The only way to travel on the tube was to stand in a corner with the newspaper wrapped around two sides of me furiously reading it cover to cover and even then it was necessary to jump off at every stop some days and wait for the next train. The problem was constantly picking up the feelings of other passengers around me. They vibrated fear and it was important to learn how to make barriers. At that time all was exacerbated by the constant alert for an Irish IRA bomb, this problem caused the tube trains to be stopped for long times in the tunnel between stations, or the commuters were herded into a station corridor for a long time.

When the going gets tough, the best answer for me is always to hold my nose and jump into everything I feared. The only way is forward, there is no other way; you can't go back and you can't just stop still.

Chapter Fifteen

Logic will get you from A to Z but imagination will take you everywhere

Albert Einstein

To manifest the life you wish for, make a complete picture of what you desire in life right down to the smallest detail. See it, feel it, smell it, see what you are wearing, what your surroundings are and just keep walking forward, sooner or later you will walk around a corner onto the next page in your life and it will be there. Do not waiver. We make our lives in the way we wish. The only thing to curb us is ourselves. How do you think some people make it and others don't? They never doubt; they expect the opportunities to arrive for them, so they do. They are the ones who recognise the banana that turned up was for them and not the apple they requested, so they take the banana. We must expect the very best and that way we make a place for it to arrive. If you don't make a place for it, it can't arrive, can it? Whatever it is, see it, feel it, make it a reality.

If only we had the wisdom and experience in our youth that we gain with age, life would be just brilliant! Mind you if you went back to your youth with that wisdom, it would be a case of "Blow that" who would want to go back, lets just go on, youth's too painful to repeat.

It was around this time in Notting Hill that I started picking up negative energies in the flat. In the war there had been some rather unfortunate tenants. They were depressive alcoholics.

At the time I was completely unaware of the need to regularly clear the house energies. Now I do this for myself and friends. It makes an enormous difference to the buoyancy of the energy trapped in a house. All homes need to be energetically cleared on every level removing the build up of old upsets, emotions, arguments, sorrow, and depression a big difference can be made as my energy is very positive and it helps me to be such a powerful manifestor i.e. I have absolutely no doubt. I never have any doubt in what I am doing and for why. I just know that it works and so it does.

As an archetype, I am the Healer and Alchemist. For both of these you are just a clear channel of the light. Open up stand to one side and let it all through. Don't go to the dark side that's putting your power to the wrong use. All people have an archetype: the musician, the lawyer, the teacher, the administrator, the carer — whose opposite is the jailer — they all have opposites. We all slot under one or two headings, and they all have their dark and negative side try not to go there.

Never step back with doubt. Whatever you do, do it with your full power and passion, but never with force, we know what we wish to achieve but must not interfere with its means of arrival, that's a job for *The Management*. Don't doubt, just quietly know you have the power and it's yours to use. Go forward whole heartedly, that's a lovely expression, what is the use of half a heart. Never let the ego use it for the negative to gain power over another. Love without conditions that's all there is; just that nothing else.

Often in my life those who comment the most on how calm, restful and healing my house is leave a package of old emotions behind them. Still all friends are loved problems or not. What I have now put into place outside the front door is a metaphysical bin for the emotional rubbish that people pick up. Their rubbish can be deposited there and they can pick it up on the way out if it is still needed as a crutch, or it can just be looked at dispassionately and jettisoned.

It is amazing what people cart around with them through life. They are often just the sum total of their illness or problems, their upbringing — what they let everybody do to them — and what they should or must do. It's as if they don't exist as a being and are only alive as a walking problem or condition. It's their whole life and crutch, and to drop it all is like putting the child's clingy toy in the washing machine. They become transfixed. It is their whole life, but it does stop you from walking forward. The thought is always present that "Nothing ever works for me, I always have bad luck etc." These people are needy. What a total waste of a potential for this life! Who knows what seeds we hold within us and what magic might come forth if we remember to project the life we want to have? If we don't project it the universe can't supply it, because it all works in this dimension via the laws of attraction.

My role in life is to just be here as a sounding board for others as they speak out. Hopefully they receive back and understand that they receive their own answers from themselves. A trouble shared is an old but true adage. Sometimes I will pass a message on to people but it only comes from their greater selves they just don't listen they are in denial, but it's not my words and I have no prior knowledge of what I might say to people at any time, and do not remember afterwards what I have said. When sharing a problem out loud to a friend you arrive at your own answers, no one knows you and what you want and need, as much as you your self do.

The answer is not to be found in another. It's the same as self care; you are your own best mother. You instinctively know what you really want and how to provide it. Don't hang around and look to others, nurture yourself and clear yourself. One of the ways to lose your way and cloud your energies, is to involve yourself in one emotional/physical relationship after another, with no time for self healing and clearing between them all.

We all need time to discover who we are — now. We change and we develop through each relationship with another, so time is needed to retrench and to get to know ourselves again first, before we embark on the next relationship. This way we will come to know and develop respect for ourselves helping to reassess our own life's journey.

All relationships are a learning curve and if we hurtle forward with no clearing time in between each one we are on the route to disaster, we will be carrying the emotional baggage from the previous relationship's to fed into the next. It is not commonly realised that when starting another close emotional or sexual relationship, because of the spiritual and physical closeness you will pick up the residue of that other person's previous partners' life's collected junk.

We have a lot of our inherited family history including all its situations of negative possession etc. these particularly can continue for many generations. Our spirit, as well as our physical genes, becomes faulty with time. All these things leave a grey residue to contend with, this can remain in the energetic body for a very long time, clouding and slowing up the spiritual development.

Steps need to be taken to clear in both the physical and spiritual dimension. It's the difference between the clear vibrational sound of striking a true note or the clunk of a cracked bowl. Clearing can be as simple as, burning sage and taking a bath in salt water, or with the correct help, opening the Akashic records and enquiring if there are things from past lives that need to be addressed and cleared energetically in this one.

Negative possession is harder it needs the full cooperation and desire to oust whatever has taken up residence everything can be cleared if ones highest guides are called in, the good will always oust the bad, It is in this dimension that clearing and development can be accomplished but it must be fully desired in the here and now.

We, and all things we relate to, are connected. It's simply stage one of quantum physics. There are no barriers and we can communicate with all things and vice versa. It would be a great help to our spiritual development if we learned how to each clear and heal ourselves Physically, Energetically and Spiritually, none of these things can be separated. You would clean and clear your home every time you move house, so do the same after all the drama of break-ups and misunderstandings in relationships. Don't let the heavy energy stagnate, clear your home and surroundings every few months. Don't let emotional rubbish build up in the corners — let in the light.

Adolescent's rooms, if you can get into them, will benefit from a clearing they can get very heavy on the emotional front, doing this small thing will help them to progress faster in a higher vibrational environment that will help with the major brain reconfiguration that occurs at this period. In fact, clear everything second-hand that comes into the house as everything carries the energy of its previous owner or place.

Chapter Sixteen

Be the change you wish to see in the world.

Gandhi

THE early seventies came along and we were a happily growing family in Notting Hill, surrounded by many friends from all walks of life. We were all young then, making our way and earning a living. Many have gone on to fame fortune and the four corners of the world.

A short while ago, there was a strange experience that came from the now distant past, it was when an American friend in France was moving back to New York and I told her you simply must find an old Notting Hill friend of mine called Joyce, a painter. She went back to the USA at least thirty-five years ago. When my friend rang me a few months after her arrival, I asked her if she found Joyce "Oh yes" she said I found her the first day of looking it was without really trying. My friend was astonished that this happened but I wasn't as I knew that these two friends have things to contribute to each others lives, it was just important for them to meet up, for what or why who knows? I am of the opinion that you will find the proverbial needle in the haystack, if you really want to and totally expect to, I had a fine example of this when, one day, running after my dog on a stoney beach, I grabbed him then realised that the car keys had dropped some way back. I had to have them so I walked back with a strong intention, not panic that I would find them and I did. They were in the stones.

Many things have been found this way, by being totally single-minded and trying hard enough, we can recall everything we do if we are determined to. It is still all there in our memory, it helps if we also remember to ask our guides to find things with us.

After nine years of Notting Hill life in our basement flat, the landlord died, with this we gained an opportunity to move on, the new landlord promptly offered us a small amount of money to go. We thought about it, and then jumped at the chance to buy a house, as we were now four in what was basically a two room flat. The prices of London houses at that time were ludicrously low in unfashionable areas, compared to the elevated price of now. We tramped around many parts of London and settled on a three bed semi in Brixton, it was opposite the gates leading to the beautiful Brockwell Park.

The house was a Victorian semi-detached in yellow brick with stucco trim, it was set well back from the road with a front garden and a one hundred and fifty foot rear garden. At last, I was about to re-acquaint myself with nature, after a very long separation.

The first way to proceeded was to make a garden for us and the children this involved removing heaps of old junk, stoves, beds etc., plus miles of barbed wire, that in time was replaced by rambling roses — a much more effective barrier. We then made a big vegetable garden and workshop. There we were in almost central London with a vast park opposite and all home-grown vegetables with fruiting apple and pear trees perfect.

The next thing to be done was to acquire a dog for the family. So with that in mind when on a short stay with a friend in Berkshire, we returned on the train with a six-month dog on a string. He was a beautiful, glittering black short haired Pointer, Labrador cross we called him Oska.

Oska was the first of many dogs; he made a good addition to the family as having a dog involved daily walking in the vast park full of mature trees. The park gate's were just across the road from us, so it was also a place where the children were able to swim with John in the open air lido, before going on to school. As far as my son was concerned this helped to remove excess energy in the play park on the way home, it was a good place to be with children and we flourished, and happily stayed in Brixton for twelve years.

1972 came and an old friend from the film business and her artist husband decided to up sticks from Notting Hill, and move to Suffolk, they bought an old farmhouse, formally a ruined monastery with many outbuildings, plus three acres of land. They all needed help with restoration. That then was the future family holidays sorted.

Not having a car yet, we took the train with the children, dog and bags for a summer fortnight, plus Easter as well for some years. The children now had a link to the country, in a house that was big enough for them to have their own bedrooms and all the advantages of a second home with an extended family.

The house in Suffolk was always full of artists and people from the film world. As far as the eye could see it was surrounded by the wonderful Suffolk countryside, and the coast was near enough to explore. I spent most of my holiday time weeding, pruning and cutting my way through a jungle outside with trees growing through the barns and the garden buried under brambles. For me it was paradise. I was well in touch with the earth and that made my holidays.

After the move to Brixton and through a chance connection -are any by chance? — life changed. The opportunity arose to do interior designing and also a connection that led to me to installing the massive Christmas window displays in central London. In continuation from this, I took on the styling of photographic sets for major paint and wallpaper companies. Although this work involved a lot of studio work, being freelance meant my hours could be juggled. Commuting up and down on southern region trains until the Victoria underground line opened in Brixton High Street.

All of this was an opportunity to expand into what I was trained for. Nothing ever learned has gone to waste; everything has turned out to be yet another stepping stone to leap from one thing into something new.

On looking back on my life, the interlinking pattern is clear to see and it's all been such fun. There has never been a time that I haven't worked. It was mostly freelance to accommodate children, John and the ongoing building projects. My money paid for cars, furniture, holidays — the extras in life.

I was born with far too much energy and passion for life, to enjoy the experience of staying at home being the happy housewife. Being at full stretch is what I am happy with. My life has been spent working in many strange occupations, as well as being in working relationships with a diverse cross section of people. Many that I have washed up against over the years have contributed a lot towards my understanding, of people's interaction with each other.

As well as being an old soul, I hope that I have learnt a great deal this time around, because this was my intention for my return. Earth is a wonderful place and full of opportunity for the taking, if one can remain flexible concerning the outcome.

Brixton was a good place to live; the preponderance of West Indian settlers in the Borough gave us wonderful street markets that were a source of constant discovery, on both the music and food front plus, the general good-natured repartee. I really miss this in my new life it's a long way from then and a long way from there.

Looking backward is like flying low over a landscape. You are involved, but not involved, just a benign onlooker with a feeling of "If only I had known that then". One thing that I have noticed is the amount of my good friends now who have lived very near me at other times but we were unaware of each other; just passing and not making a hit rather like planets passing.

The children had a multiracial schooling with mixed results as discipline was a bit slack, but they have retained their acceptance of all races and colours and in turn it is passed on to the grandchildren. This pleases me as in my upbringing there was never the slightest tinge of racism. I wish such attitudes were worldwide. The fear that we have on seeing another person who looks or sounds a little different from ourselves, is holding us back. All human emotions boil down to either love or fear, mostly the latter. Whereas we should be stepping forward and embracing the difference as all variations add to our personal and our world development.

We are living on such a small planet but our resources are enough for everyone, if only we combined our knowledge for the good of all, and not just for one-upmanship and personal profit making. Humans think that they are so superior and advanced but it must be a constant source of disappointment to other more advanced beings that humans are still so primitive. They are passionate about their differences and borders with an attitude of "What's mine is mine and I will have yours as well if I can get it off you". Constantly bickering about border's and waving they're silly flags! Constantly, fighting, like small boys.

As far as the world situation goes, we are all fiddling about waiting until Mummy tells us what to do. She's not there. Just do what you can do. Start with your own life, disregard whether others are pulling their weight or not, just stand up and be counted, try to remember the glorious beings that we all have the potential to be. It's got to start sometime, and it's got to start somewhere.

We really do all have to get out of the spiritual kindergarten sometime soon, before we destroy the magnificent world that was both our gift, and the next generation's birthright. We are at a pivotal point in our development and all will collapse inward sooner or later, as all things do when they have been built on a rotting base of lies.

So much help has been given to us, from the other dimensions, there is an immense amount of goodwill towards us but we are too occupied by the minutiae of life to connect with the reality of the greater picture of the real life. We are sucked into a maelstrom of negativity and reaction instead of coming from a place of pro-action. There is no such thing as individual governments, now we have a world government of big business and banking linking behind the scenes of everything. The world is governed from a place of divide, those that have risen to the top, instil fear and a feeling of neediness to the general public. Now everybody thinks that they need something, whatever it might be this keeps them "needy" and distracted from the greater picture of what is really going on in the world.

Loose the blueprint of the past as it will not create the future that we want and need now. The way the world has been organised up until now has not exactly been a success, so why keep on repeating it. The rich have not exactly ploughed their excess profit back into the economy they just put it off-shore to generate even more. We are the co-creators, so create a world we can be proud to pass on.

Chuck out the excess baggage of outdated ideas. If they didn't work before they are not going to work in the future, are they?

We are now and have always been given "bread and circuses for the masses" even the Romans did that — stop them starving and entertain them, then they won't revolt. We are still being given it, yet again and again. It keeps people occupied servicing their individual debt and all of their spare time is spent shopping. They are addicted to shopping and think it will fill the needy hole in the solar plexus. It won't, that way it will only increase people's indebtedness reducing them to being a wage slaves forever.

No other country is going to overpower us physically now there are far more subtle ways to achieve this, we are already ruled from the countries and banks that we are in the most debt to. It is because we have relinquished the control of our future to those who only seek personal profit and so now in the situation that they have stepped in and taken over from us. Leave a vacuum and it will be filled nature abhors a vacuum, and this works on all levels in life, if we continue to let ourselves be dominated by those who only look after their own financial interests, then we deserve to be treated like the fools we have become.

The time has come for each individual to set themselves free from an existence dominated by fear, remove attention from the high drama of, fear of war, fear of famine, and fear of financial catastrophe. We would do better to starve these things of the attention they desire, as giving them attention makes them a reality and gives them power. Things can only have power over us and make us fearful and stuck like a rabbit, in the headlights, if we wish it to be like this, so take your energy from it. The time has come when we must walk forward boldly and put this wasted energy into creating the world we desire to inhabit. First, replace fear and judgement with love and forgiveness. The later is important to apply to ourselves first.

Life is just a short dream remember, and we are just a very small part of our greater selves on an experiencing and learning trip.

The natural world cannot fear evil, and the animals have no conception of it. I have no conception of evil coming to us from the outside, as it can only exist when we recognise it. My thoughts are more in-line with quantum physics. We are the ones to manifest evil, if we put out a fear of evil we give it life, as everything we put out is reflected back to us, — the universe will only supply you with "nothing works for me" if that's what you put out for. We will always receive what we consciously or subliminally put out for, so be very careful what you spend your time allowing to come in your head, as thought's make your reality.

Fear is a way of control; if you can make your neighbour fearful you have control over them, fear is a powerful weapon, think of a field of sheep when one is startled they all panic, don't be a sheep, access the situation and go forward with your gut feeling. The more people who bring in the light and the calm view of the world the better, step forward from the panicking mass, in this way we will help to tip the balance into a more positive and loving direction.

Be very, very careful in both your thoughts and your words. This practice applies to all things. Think you can't do something and you can't. Think you're not worth a good job and you won't be. Think you are addicted to something and you are.

WORDS MAKE YOUR REALITY: so be very careful what you think. You are your own creator and if you see yourself as a victim so you will be. If you expect bad luck so it will be. This is how we manifest.

First learn to love and forgive yourself and expect the best for you and it will be, because you become attuned to seeing the opportunity and you will take it. You will see that you are in the right place at the right time. Don't be a victim or think that something has a hold over you. If you do, you will sink and make such turmoil in the process you will miss the many subtle opportunities that are ready to link in with you each day.

Chapter Seventeen

Plans are useless, but planning is indispensable.

Eisenhower

WE lived in Brixton for many years. The children finished schooling and passed on to other things, further education and going out into the world in the normal way of the constant changing family requirements.

The next move came along suddenly, in the now serendipitous way it always does in my life. It happened when we were driving back and forth through the Kennington back streets. One day we noticed a small sign on a tinned up unoccupied house, it was being sold off by the council as it was one they were not allowed to knock down for historic reasons.

The house overlooked Kennington Park a place that witnessed great historical events, the major one being the 10 April 1848 Chartist rally, calling for justice and an increase in working class starvation wages.

From the house it was a quick walk to Walworth Road market and the tube station. The price was low as tramps had occupied the house for years; the tramps had taken both the lead off the roof, and removed the doors and fireplaces, leaving it sad and semi-derelict.

As the windows were tinned up, we viewed it in the darkness with a torch, and we fell for it, bang. It was a case of go on let's do it one more time; it's such fun and it desperately needs rescuing. Some people rescue cats, and some houses, what fools we always were always falling for money pits of wrecked houses. I think we just aided and abetted each other. But I do know that we have left a trail of beautifully restored houses behind us, and we enjoyed the processes of doing them even if it used up all our time and money, we were obviously on a restoration of places things and people this time around

So there it was a beautiful, plain Georgian house, four storeys with two rooms per floor. The exquisite plasterwork mouldings were wet, the doors and fireplaces stolen. It was just a shell but glorious in its proportions and balance. The Golden Mean, the ancient geometrical system of both measurement and proportion, there in its glory- in bricks and mortar.

Having fallen for the house, there was no alternative but to buy it at once. We instantly found a buyer for our house that evening, this is typical of my life, it always just rockets forward on occasion with such a gee-force and me clutching on. So we started on our final, London major renovation project of the derelict house in Kennington. Nearly all the work of renovation we did ourselves whilst at the same time, working full time at our jobs. The children had flown the nest moving on to their own choices of lives paths.

The day we moved in to the semi converted house, the Falkland war had started. The floors were odd sheets of board on joists; we had no bathroom or lavatory, except for in the park across the road, thieves had broken in and stolen a small portable TV so we never saw the war! Good! The sight of humans still killing themselves and the newspapers cheering on the deaths of teenagers just out of school, is just too depressing — nothing changes after all this time.

Our dog was a young Wolfhound/Deer-hound cross, the first of many, her name was Tussie, and she became adept at walking over floor joists. She spent most of her time watching John laying floors, and was fascinated by it. This made me realise that all young animals automatically learn whatever life skills are necessary from the leader of the pack, the one who is the top dog. So there we were, a dog who could possibly lay a floor! That in itself should help us to understand the importance of learning the traditional way an apprentice at the side of an older person — watch one done — do one — and then teach one — as the saying goes.

The house was a small, but beautiful house, and it was almost possible to walk into the centre of London on a Sunday to see the exhibitions and whatever new was going on. From the top back window of the house I could see the dome of St Paul's Cathedral. It was a convenient place for getting to work straight down the main road to Wandsworth.

The house was a simple semi-detached house with a square spiral staircase up through the centre. The garden was small, but sunny and secluded so I had fun creating a new small garden. It was here in this garden, that John built his first conservatory; a small hexagonal one this time. This was to be the first of many conservatories of different sizes and shapes; all little palaces he built for me. We were in a physically overstretched condition, we now owned the house — a shell — in Kennington, plus a stake in a holiday house set high up on the cliffs at Hastings, the latter was shared with two other families.

As well as the two houses I had a half-share with a male friend in a rented shop in Wandsworth where we ran an interior design business. I was back to designing interiors and sewing for my living but the only problem with having a shop was that I had to work on alternate Saturdays. What was so odd about the shop was that thirty years later when I was living in France I met the mother of a friend who was brought up just across the road from the shop and clearly remembered going to buy a cake there on Saturdays when it was still a bakery

The friend who shared the business with me was yet another male from a past life. Before we met up, he appeared in a dream standing next to my bed, asking me to help him — they nearly all turn up like this asking for my help. I remember a feeling of Oh bother! and saying "All right then" in a rather reluctant way, it was like discovering a job not finished. We had obviously made a karmic arrangement prior to meting up for a short time, one often makes small promises of this type prior to coming into this dimension, and I appear to have made many.

Roger came into my life shortly after the dream; he was in a very unhappy relationship with a photographer that I was working with at the time. When I was asked to design and furnish a London house for a very well-known film director, I immediately asked him to do the upholstery. He was rather difficult with a fiery disposition and by no means easy to work with being that his politics were far right at the time and he could be rather nasty and racist. We opened a shop and worked together for about five years it was not always easy, as temperamentally we were very different. He was very fiery as well as having the drama of his rather complex homosexual private life.

There we go steep learning curves as usual, over the few years we were together though he mellowed, and was of a happy disposition.

I often don't have an easy time with people who come in my life for a time and a purpose but if I stick it out it is rewarding and I will always have a deep fondness for him.

After three years of living in Kennington, John with many others at that time took early retirement and we decided to move on, even though the Kennington house was going to be so perfect and quiet for living in London. John fancied off again, and this time it was to involve leaving the city for good. When the opportunity came up for him to leave he did, the senior lecturers of universities were being thinned out from the top to make room for the younger ones to rise, he was a brilliant teacher but burnt out by teaching and wanted to paint write and bind books, plus fall madly in love with more ruined houses perhaps.!

The lease for the shop conveniently came to an end shortly before so the business was closed. After my business partner Rodger and I parted amicably I had another dream of him. Yet again he stood by my bed and thanked me. What is so odd about the two dreams is I clearly remember the shirt he was wearing. It was the same each time; a khaki shirt, never am I able to remember him wearing a khaki shirt in this life?

Soon after our move to the country, he joined the many others of that time who succumbed to the Aids virus; He died very painfully and very young. I still really miss his wonderful, super-sharp wit but we obviously were just meant to touch base for a short time in this dimension and had achieved what we had arranged to do. He was at a difficult time in his life, that all resolved over our few years together, but who he was in relation to me I never asked although he felt like he had been a brother to me.

Some people have been in my life four or five times previously and my relationships with them can get a bit confusing when finding myself slipping into previous familial roles, brother, lover, son, or father, and so many were sisters and old female friends. I must not forget to be in the present and remember what role it is to be in the here now.

We sold the part we owned of the house in Hastings which was sad as it was a treat to drive down to the sea late on Friday night, take the dog for a walk on the beach and live with no connections for the weekend. Just walk on the cliffs and eat fish. For me the winter is particularly suited to walking on the beach, wrapped in a coat, just breathing the salt air and walking the dog. It's the only time that I feel really alive, how I miss the sea, I am very far inland now.

If it was a feasible choice, my life would always be lived by the sea. Just put it down to my Frisian/English ancestry. To lie on the beach in the off-season is heaven for me. The sound and smell are extraordinarily healing and I almost feel a part of the sea.

I now find that with the high vibration essence making and the healing work that I do it is very difficult to exist in or visit a city.

The vibrational levels of the inhabitants are so dense that they hardly vibrate at all. Their resonance is very muffled. My guides tell me that the essences that I make today will be of great help to the overstressed people in the future as we all go through the vibrational transition. We will see all is part of the road of discovery and work in progress, I am constantly told by my guides to have patience, just do my part and they will take care of the rest. My part is the manifesting, only a person living in this dimension can manifest for this dimension.

Chapter Eighteen

We are not human beings having a spiritual experience,
we are spiritual beings having a human experience.

TAILHARD CHARDIN

WELL, footloose as usual we thought let's make a run for it and move to East Anglia. John's family came from Suffolk, and for many years we had taken the family and stayed with our friends in an old Abbey in the heart of the Suffolk countryside. This was when we made our first bad move swayed by a golden handshake and the high London price we received for our house. What did we do but fall in love with and then bought, a white elephant of a house — all a bit of a repeat from my childhood.

The house was large with a walled garden, it was very beautiful and built in the late Queen Anne/Early Georgian period, it had five roofs full of dry rot and many other horrors to put right, it was a money pit, a financial drain, so the money certainly ran through our fingers fast. But it was wonderful it had four vast reception rooms the smallest being twenty-five feet each way — very cold in the winter. At one end of the building was a grand ballroom that had been turned into an Edwardian kitchen containing a massive mechanical cooking range, the latter was promptly dispatched to a local national Trust property.

Amongst its many attributes the house turned out to be rather haunted but not nastily. An elderly lady informed me, in the street one day, that when she was a girl it was owned by a gentleman who ran a silk works, and he was inclined to entertain ladies of ill repute — that's a wonderful term and explained a lot. I had been walking into rooms filled with a strong scent of heavy perfume, there was also a distinct cloud of cigar smoke on the stairs that one unexpectedly ran through from time to time, that's not the first time I've encountered things on the stairs, perhaps because they are a transit place.

Poor Isabel, my sister, stayed the night in an odd shaped unused room at the rear of the house, the first night that she stayed she was tossed out of bed by three children. We since found out that the room she slept in was the old nursery before it had been cut up for remodelling the house, the children had all died of scarlet fever a few of generations back, they obviously did not want her in there.

It was whilst living in this house that a premonition of my future and of the link it would have with my old lives came up. I did not realise at the time that all was beginning to unfold into a future that would prove to be so hard to live through, rather like seeing a distant land across the bay with the reefs to tackle before landing on the far shoreline. The hardest bit was yet to come.

My sister Isabel is a sensitive like me, one of her skills was being able to hold something and tell about it — without seeing it. She would say where it came from and why it was here, also who owned it. Well, one day when walking along an upper landing I picked up a beautiful, fabric-covered, handmade, ancient but absolutely spotless button. It was lying right in the middle of the floor immaculate — it had never been used or touched, I gave it to Bell to hold without her first seeing it. Immediately she said you are wearing a long dark blue dress, you are in France with many other women all would be well, that took me back having no intention of going to France only having had a brief experience of Paris and at that time and I was not very fond of the natives.

The button is still with me somewhere to this day. At that time, I was ignorant of my Cathar history and the fact of it being the most meaningful incarnation I had had so far. OK! Things had started coming through and there was lots more to come, with a much different life for me than ever could have been imagined; also, it was just around the corner.

This was not to be the first occasion of coming across immaculate things, manifesting into my life untouched by hands, much later when John had died, I had bought a new book on line, it arrived newly printed and shrink-wrapped in polythene, It was a book on quantum physics that fact in itself was significant, as I ran through the pages a twenty pound note fell out it was a strange one it was so new and had not come out of a bank machine in fact it had just been printed and nobody had ever touched it, I had an absolute knowing then and now that it was real and was sent to me as a token of Johns care and future provision for me. On finding the money, the thought came to me at once, of a statement that he had made when very ill and I had been running backwards and forwards after him, laughing and saying who will look after me in my old age, he laughed back and replied in all seriousness, the memory of the statement resonates, that he would look after me of course and he has ever since, all things appear as soon as they are thought about leaving me never in a place of need.

The beautiful house and garden in Suffolk were completed over many years. Later, when opening the garden for charity one day, a man who was to become good friend in the future visited the garden after receiving a phone call from his excited brother. His name was Mike the man who founded of Neal's Yard whole- foods in Covent garden London, and had moved up to Suffolk. He viewed the garden at the end of the day, was impressed and asked me there and then if I would go and work with him at a very special plant nursery that he was in the process of setting up — and was to be called Woottens. I looked at him and thought why not and as usual an instant decision was made you only have to ask me once. I turned to John and said "What about it", as usual he said "Why not, do as you want, you will enjoy it".

I was to start a new life, yet again, surrounded by all the beautiful plants that were loved so well, we worked together contentedly building the nursery for some years, little did I imagine that a much different future was about to open, all was not heading for indefinite calm, there were other plans afoot for me!

One night a mysterious dream came — I am a very significant dreamer — the dream was of a plant called Inula Helenium, so having an idea that this was a plant that I needed at that time, I became obsessed, which is always a dangerous sign, searching through all my books then finding the plant eventually in an old herbal that John had bought me many years ago.

What was so strange was that he would buy me a book and its significance was not recognised at the time but it would play a pivotal role in my life in the future, looking backwards he was always unwittingly behind the movements that were to point me eventually into my life's most significant role —perhaps it wasn't unwittingly — he was with me in this dimension to get me to a certain place at a certain time in my life, often his drawings were of something that would appear in my future life, he was a very private man and never ever discussed such things with me.

Reading the herbal book avidly from cover to cover rapidly becoming totally obsessed the penny dropped. I wanted to study herbalism as that was what had interested me as a very small child. Then in my usual full speed ahead manner, as chance always has it in my life, the very next week at the yoga classes when talking with the teacher who was soon to be friend, she told me that she was attending part-time one of the best herbal schools in the country and it was in easy reach. This is the way I manifest, I only have to wish to do something powerfully and everything drops into place at great speed.

Promptly I stopped my job at the nursery and began studying herbs not realising at the time that this was to be one of the most profound things in my life. I spun around and was going at full speed in a different direction picking up the thread from old and what were to become all to familiar lives.

After many years in the big house, it was a case of here we go again, John decided that he was not happy in the heart of the country and wanted to move nearer to Norwich, on reflection this was fine by me as I was missing the cultural aspect of life on my doorstep, so off we went again. The sale of the house was very difficult as the market had dropped and we had borrowed money to finish it, this was the first time we had lost money but the times then were bad for everybody, we eventually sold it at a low price and stayed between houses for six months renting a flat by the seaside, whilst carefully searching for a suitable new home.

Eventually we found a good medium-sized house in a small market town, it was not far south of Norwich, and just what we wanted, except that the garden was over-large, my department yet again — How many more gardens are to be in my life? — I've not stopped yet.

The land was full of fruit trees as the previous people had grown the fruit commercially. I made a large vegetable garden and we kept a moveable pen with half a dozen bantam's this we moved up and down the rows of raised vegetables garden producing instant compost from our waste food, I loved my bantam's, and was reminded at this time of an ancient aunt of John's who in the war had kept chickens, one bird that was a prolific layer was having trouble with some grit that had caught in the gullet his aunt then proceeded to put the bird under her arm cut open its gullet removed the grit and stitched it up again, off it went none the worse for its operation.

Unbeknown to us, John was more than worn out by the work on the last house because he was a being who hardly felt pain we were totally unaware that he had had a massive stomach ulcer developing with an internal bleed, he thought he was just having a bit of tiredness and indigestion.

Two weeks after we moved into this new house I was woken up in middle of the night by a shout ran downstairs and found him lying on the kitchen floor in a rapidly spreading pool of blood, it was unstoppable, the time was two in the morning, so he was rushed to hospital for the first of the major disasters, this time for an emergency operation for an enormous stomach ulcer, that had eroded into the pancreas and was rupturing the main artery he was like a blood fountain continuously vomiting blood,

He was given bags and bags of blood; I still don't know and neither does anybody else, who was there at the time, know how he survived. He obviously just had to be in the world, there was no alternative. "See you soon" he said, fooling about euphorically waving a sick bowl like a top hat as he was wheeled behind the curtain and rushed into surgery and his expected death.

The memory of that night is very clear; it was the time that I stepped forward into the power of my greater self. None of us know who we

are until the time comes and the realisation of whom and what we are overpowers us, all doubt is brushed aside.

I was sitting alone in the emergency waiting room in the middle of the night. Suddenly and without a thought I got up from my seat in such a confident way as if knowing exactly what was to be done, I crossed the room and moved to put my back to the wall in a corner, then bringing the power up through my body from under the earth, I said with every ounce of my of desire "I need help on this one and I need it now" there was nothing polite about my request, no please or thank you I will try harder to be better, it was a total and powerful demand — with no doubt.

Help came immediately with a great surge of heat from my feet upwards, I was viewing John horizontal in front of me on a table surrounded by a brilliant flashing gold outline he looked as if he was in a golden sarcophagus, all my links in every dimension were called in and they all responded instantaneously, that was the first time in this life that I had consciously stepped forward into my power and manifested with complete and absolute confidence. It was so powerful I was totally convinced that it would work — and it did.

Now I do know this will happen with anyone who steps forward with total belief, absolute conviction. We all have the ability to manifest, one must never doubt for one instant. Doubt and it will cut your intention off at the feet, be totally unshakeable and just know whatever it is, it's yours for the demanding. It no longer amazes me as it's so familiar, I'm now aware that it was not the time for him to go yet; his job, although not realising it then, was to take and settle me in France first.

The following day my sister rang and said she had been awake all night doing healing work helped by someone with very pale blue eyes, later we were to find out who he was. He came into her life and went on to be her new partner, when he came into her life one of the first things he talked of was being woken in the night and working with gold but for whom or what he did not know — he was also a healer.

This is a perfect example of the automatic ability we all have to connect, there are no gaps or time between us, all sensations just flow between us. Distance is irrelevant we could be on another planet, it is instantaneous when the power behind the intention has no doubt or negativity attached to it. I often send my energetic essences across the world by intention alone and they are received.

Animals communicate with each other and us in silence and honesty but as we developed the skills of communicating by language we learnt to hide behind it, lies can be told using language and our real feelings can be hidden. We then start to separate from our own feelings and those of others, we can make ourselves hidden and different, we can form into groups, tribes and countries and even planets, we can become separate. As it goes — divide and you rule — you fear the other and you instil fear in the other.

We are just one giant conglomeration we are all an aspect and part of the great creative source — there are many names for this but only one source — joined without a start or finish — whatever we think or do we are one.

The majority of humans now live behind veils of secrecy, in fact we love secrets, they keep us in fear and add to the stress that we are so addicted to, they keep us separate. Don't tell this, don't tell that, every secret adds yet another division another layer and makes yet another subgroup, secrets encourage the darkness, and fear of the unknown.

What can be secret about emotions or thoughts, they are felt by all there is no emotion feeling or thought that can be new and as we are totally connected to each other and our source what's to hide, guilt embarrassment, shame, all these things are very human and hold us back, there is only one thing to be careful with and that's information that is likely to hurt another.

The thing to try next time when in a difficult or hurtful situation, is to just almost physically lift and place ego to one side then communicate from the heart its very simple to do, when you have done it once you realise that it makes everything clear and easy. It's impossible to hurt the soul, only the ego can be hurt; on occasion I think of the ego as a ten-year-old boy standing in front of me spoiling for a fight with fists ready to defend me to the end. Ego is very panicky terrified that you won't need him, just kindly put him aside sometimes, and say "It's OK, I will deal with this now" and go forward from the heart.

Chapter Nineteen

Where there is love, there is life

Mahatma Gandhi

AT the time of Johns first operation I was working as a herbalist from my dispensary at home, but soon I decided to go and work in Norwich at an alternative health centre that was just a short drive away. This suited me well and all was going just fine, we were enjoying the house and the extensive garden.

After a while John slowly became yellow and after checks another operation was needed for clearing the bile duct that had blocked solid in the initial ulcer rupture. This turned out to be major surgery and a stent was inserted, it was a disaster the hospital was very dirty and after the surgery the care was very haphazard, he contracted a major hospital infection causing gangrene.

It was at this time that I took my first controversial step to save his life and take over the responsibility for him. His gangrene infection resulted in an extraordinarily high temperature. When visiting the hospital one day I found that he was suffering from such rigour the bed shook; he was not being cooled or cared for, the floor was filthy with puss, the curtains were closed they had left him, and they had expected him to die.

After arguing with the doctors we agreed that he stay in to finish a course of intravenous antibiotics they then gave him, I told them that he would then be taken from the hospital as it was no place for a sick person, I would be responsible for him, on the whole they were grateful as they did not want the blame for a death to fall on their heads. I took responsibility from that day on, if ever he was in hospital ever again I stayed around the clock and never left him until he was stable.

When he came home he was in an appalling state, almost skeletal with a fistula, I put him in a small room, covered everything with clean white sheets and feed him around the clock with very small amounts of a limited cleansing diet. His bed faced a window that overlooked the trees, and I treated him with my herbal skills. Thank goodness for the amazing teachers that had taught me. I had never doubted myself, nursing him around the clock using all the skill and power I could muster, I did not realise at the time that this was to be a situation that was to repeat itself many times for the rest of his life for the next ten years or so.

John recovered, or so we thought, and to prove himself fit again, he celebrated by building on to the back of the house a very large and beautiful conservatory. We were happy but unaware, at the time, that he was to be a ticking time bomb with only a few years grace.

Well, here we go again it's getting very regular now, he sat at the table one Christmas day and said that he would like to live in the centre of Norwich so as usual it was OK, and I went along with the idea.

Looking back I realise that it was always me that went along with what he suggested, yet I am a very independent person really, but he as usual was irresistible in his enthusiasm for a new project and my feet are always itchy from childhood house moving. I also just like making people happy, so if there is no good valid reason to say no, OK! just go for it who knows where it might lead always rely on the gut reaction and jump.

The day after, Boxing Day came and we meet the house agent and set to doing a bit of very rapid finishing painting around the house so it could go on the market at the start of January. The first viewing was to be the second of January. This was to get me painting and clearing through the night before in fact I backed myself into the cellar took the paint splashed-clothes off, washed and changed, I had no sleep, but was ready for the first appointment.

The viewer came along at nine o'clock and accepted the house at the full price, wow we had made up the money that was lost on the last white elephant disaster house — the agents photographs had not even got into his window.

This time we found what was to become our last house in England, it was an arts and crafts designed house, near the river on the southern edge of Norwich. This enabled me to walk into the city centre and work at the alternative health centre. Also, being near the river I was able to take the dog on a river walk in the mornings.

We were very settled for a couple of years, as well as a garden we had an allotment. John did his usual house alterations, he made a beautiful circle pergola and a hexagonal summer house made of glass and mirrors this time.

Every house he turned into a palace. A week after we married we had only just moved into a two-room flat when he started ripping down rubbishy workmanship and improving things, really he was a human form of a bower-bird always providing me with beautiful homes. It was his art form: drawing pictures and restoring furniture, as well as, writing and teaching politics, economics, in fact a renaissance man personified. Never happy if not working with both hand and brain, and ready for the next challenge. At least life was always a wonderful challenge, we always lived in the day from that time on, as tomorrow always might have been his last day.

After living in Norwich for three years we took a four-day trip to Italy and loved it; we came back and decided to rent the house out so we could go to live in Italy for six months so as not to be a passing tourist and to have a good look around. OK! sounds a good way to experience it, instead of being just on holiday, not quite what I had in mind for my life but OK! as I have said before, I am always up for having a go at anything, in fact I am more likely to say yes than no — so why not try?

We do know it is counterproductive to think too much in the long term, so keep plans flexible. Get too rigid and the guides step in and say, "Now you do remember this was not in your soul plan, think again".

I now know that my plan was to be living and working in France in the area of my old place of work that was in my most fulfilling incarnation. To achieve that, I now see that there was so much going on behind the scenes, many serendipitous manoeuvres were involved in getting me into the right position for the rest of my life. Often I look back with astonishment at how it was all achieved, one can only marvel at it all in retrospect every little thing was directed towards this end.

Well, we found tenants on a Sunday morning just as the photo was being put into the agents window; they rushed around at once and were hanging over the front gate. As I have said before this nearly always happens when wanting to do something that's on my soul path, things move so fast it's as if I am on a speeding skate board. I now know that when manifesting it is important to think very carefully first, as well as going by gut feelings, as my manifesting thought is instant in its effect very often.

Off we went to sunny Italy on our travels in a small Ford estate car, the latest wolf-hound and masses of stuff for six months. We were going to Italy to find a place to rent for an extended trip or so we thought!

Before leaving the UK we met up with an old friend who said it might be good to stop over in France and stay at a house owned by someone she met at a party as he wanted a tenant for a short time. OK! Why not? No hurry, but France was not a place that I was fond of at that time and had just learnt enough of the language to purchase some food on the way through — Italian was the language that I was learning.

We turned up at the friends recommended house, to say it was grim was an understatement, it was in the middle of a small town with no garden, It was very dark with missing windows and some rooms with no floor boards, the light-bulbs were thirty watt and we could only have one switched on at a time. I sat there and read the map by torchlight seeing how we were to get away.

The next day we delivered the owner to the airport and told him that we did not want the house. As we returned we passed Limoux, on the spur of the moment I said or rather one of my guides interjected "lets go into the town and look around". I just leave myself open to opportunities all the time

I'm obviously a walkover for them one nudge or suggestion and I'm racing ahead saying "Oh, come on let's".

We looked at a house agents window, went in and asked if they had anything to rent for a short time, as things turned out there was out of season holiday accommodation going in a village five minutes away. Without stopping for breath we drove back collected the bemused dog got our bags put the keys through the letterbox and moved into the holiday house that very evening.

The two weeks passed and we ended up staying in south-west France for eight months exploring the countryside, we never did get to Italy. It was a very strange route anyway going to Italy via South West France. What is also strange, is that I have met many others since who arrived this area on the way to other places — it's energies make it a powerful magnet.

During the last month of our stay in France we found that we were looking at houses for sale, not that we expected to buy one, but these things just creep up when you are not paying attention, we contacted our happy tenants to say that we wanted to get a valuation with a view to sell when we returned and did they mind house agents coming around. "No, on the contrary" they said "Get three, tell us a price and we will buy it".

So here we were yet again on the move. We searched for an old barn to restore; we thought that we were going to live in a caravan whilst doing the rebuilding. Oh yes? Little did we know what the future held, on occasion its best not to, but to just trust.

Those who want to make the gods laugh make plans, well it wasn't exactly like that, *The Management* were in charge again thank goodness we searched and searched for our ruin, then one day giving up hope of finding anything in our area of choice and in a state of frustration, we went by chance and saw a 1970s L-shaped bungalow. The house stood in its own grounds that ran down to a river; it had electric gates at the front, and included a very large barn that was being used as a workshop. This was never the type of house we would ever imagine us living in, we had always had Georgian or Victorian houses the youngest one being Edwardian.

Well we said yes, that was such a surprise we sat down in the garden and said a bungalow at last. How could we tell the family and friends? It was hilarious. We promptly rang the bank asked for a loan and put our ten percent down, returning to the UK later that week to put our plans in order and be ready to move in six weeks time, or so we thought!

On arriving in the UK and temporary moving back into our old house we decided to take a trip to London to see an exhibition, before starting the house packing. We stayed away for a couple of days and absorbed a bit of culture, on the return journey to East Anglia as we passed the Chelmsford bypass John felt sick leapt out of the car and vomited a copious amount of blood. With a dreadful sense of foreboding I took over the driving and we went to the nearest hospital where he was admitted and found to have varicosities in the oesophagus, the doctors informed me that he must give up drinking and he was put on beta blockers, this was not to be the last time of being faced with this comment regarding drink, I was amazed as his alcohol intake was hardly excessive. After a few days he left the hospital and we finished the journey home.

Chapter Twenty

We are not human beings having a spiritual experience,
We are spiritual beings having a human experience.

Tailhard Chardin

We started to clear the sheds and loft out as we only had four weeks to get organised. Then, one morning John sat up in bed and was very strange and unable to articulate, he would not look at me; I called the doctor who declared that he had had a stroke, so he was then taken to hospital, but after twenty-four hours of observation they accused me of bringing bottles of whisky in to him as he was drunk, this was all amazing, they tested him and the blood was clear of alcohol, so the next thing to do was a liver biopsy, his liver was infested with a very rare fungal infection only found in Pakistan or parts of America. As he had never been to America but was in Pakistan, when in the R.A.F., they came to the conclusion that it had laid dormant and had only come through with the hospital infection of some years before. John was obviously very ill, and was put on very strong antifungal medication; these with the addition of beta blockers were to cause bouts of encephalopathy for the rest of his life, affecting him long after he had given up taking them.

Although trained and working as a herbalist I was so overwhelmed at that time with the moving, needing help on every front I neglected to research the drugs thoroughly. I was later informed of the side effect that they had only after seeing a specialist after our arrival in France.

Well, there was a decision to make when he was recovering in hospital, I asked did he want to back out of the sale and forget the deposit but no he was adamant that he was going to France, so with that I returned home alone and started packing boxes the majority were finished before his homecoming. All this time I was constantly feeling that he was not right, he kept falling asleep and becoming incoherent, not realising at that time all of his efforts were to get me back to France, an arrangement made between us before we came into this incarnation together.

Moving day came around and I had no idea of the drama that was to ensue, the men came and removed the furniture, the dog was to be left with a friend for some months until John was well enough for us to drive back, we locked the door passed the keys over and drove down to Portsmouth to catch the night boat. On the way to the boat we stopped off for a snack, as we were leaving the restaurant an unexpectedly chilling foretaste of my future life came in. We sat in the car with me about to drive when he turned to me and calmly said "Right shall we go home now", I had that sudden knife in the gut feeling — Oh dear what now? So explaining to him that we had sold the house and everything was on the way to France, he calmly looked straight at me and very coldly said you really are going mad now, you need some treatment, this was said very nastily and in all seriousness.

That was to be the first real experience I had of the terrible aggressive effect on the brain that encephalopathy can have, and of what my life to come was going to be like. I was to spend my life with a man who loved me, becoming time after time without a warning an aggressive and sometimes physically violent stranger. Why was I given no advice or support? Who knows? I am able to admit to this now, at the time it was too painful to say your husband frightened you. I was very alone on my way to a strange country whose language I was unable to speak.

So we drove on with me hoping he would drop off and wake up better, already the furniture was on the boat to France and the new people had moved into our old house. There I was on the road out of the country, feeling very alone, with the one person who had always been a rock in my life, who was now a stranger, was abusive and completely unrecognisable.

We were homeless in a bizarre situation and it was about to get much worse; so I just kept walking on into the future with the hope that the page would turn soon and the next one would be better. On our arrival at the dock for the late night boat, it was only then that I discovered that the passports and tickets were with the furniture, they were packed in the dresser draw, all our papers, passports, tickets the lot, they were on the high seas by now if not in France everything was turning into a nightmare, and there was no one to turn to for advice.

Then by what was to become usual, fluke of fate? or my helpers working overtime, we were saved, as before leaving the house, the last thing I had picked up was the calendar and had thrown it in the car thinking it's too late in the season for a replacement as it was the late summer bank holiday. My sister Isabel's husband had told me to write our ticket numbers on the calendar to put them on the day of sailing, saved yet again, little did I know that my life was going to be like that from then on, dozens of helpers in the wings all manoeuvring me into place.

On approaching the harbour master with my problem he accepted the ticket numbers and informed me that "Yes one can leave the country without a passport, but cannot return without one" and the French will not accept us without one. Oh dear, holding my breath I just jumped and trusted that all would be cared for — and we would land well.

We spent a horrendous night with John getting up in the middle of it, going on a completely confused walkabout on the boat in his pyjamas saying that we were in the wrong cabin. The arrival in France was magic, it was dawn on Sunday and the dock gates were open with nobody on duty. So we just drove out into the new life.

On leaving the dock at Cherbourg, as we drove up the very steep hill out of the town I froze, and remembered that in the drama of the other side of the Channel I had forgotten to fill up with petrol and the light was now flashing, yet again my guardians leapt to the rescue. So I did a U turn and there on the last corner we had passed was a fuel station open at dawn in France on a Sunday — astounding.

All my life there is constant amazement and gratitude for all the help received when going out on a limb, and trusting my gut feeling, they are there constantly at my side, rescuing me and when necessary sweeping the path before me. This is why I walk forward through anything with total trust you must never doubt or the net will vanish, it's a bit like tightrope walking.

After that was the long drive across France and a nightmare night in a hotel with me hoping that they would not think of him as drunk when I was slipping him past the desk. A greater part of the night was spent feeding him water until the small hours, then locking the door when I desperately needed to sleep. By the next morning John had recovered, ate a big breakfast and we were able to continue south. On arrival, we drove directly to the Notaries' office with John becoming incoherent yet again and me pretending that he was very deaf and telling him repeatedly where to sign on each of the many papers.

So we were home we had arrived we were there, at the house in France and were coming to realise why we didn't get the ruined barn we were looking for obviously *The Management* knew what was going on even if I didn't so we were extremely grateful.

The furniture was due to arrive the next day; we were to make do with a blow up mattress and two garden chairs great — we had arrived. Well, we got into bed and the mattress promptly went down flat, it had a puncture. What a start to our new life here I was laying on the tiled floor with a very bizarrely behaving husband. Little did I realise then that this was to be the start of the hardest part of my life so far, it's the hardest part to write about as well.

Two days after arriving, I was thinking it might be a good idea to take the hospital notes to an interpreter, as French rather than English, would be a better for an emergency. We drove to the main square in Limoux. John insisted on waiting in the car to read the paper, on my return, he had emptied all the contents out of the car and onto the pavement. He had also opened all the doors, when asked what he was doing he replied "I'm selling the car, someone will come and buy it in a minute" Oh dear, now what? Somehow he was cajoled back in the car and driven home where he promptly fell rapidly into a coma.

The time had arrived to try the local hospital, so dragging him across the garden to the car in a plastic chair, I drove him to the hospital, where of course they said that he was a drunk, and treated my hospital letter of explanation with a Gallic shrug: "What is this so called disease?" They had never come across it before, well why should they have, they didn't have Pakistan as an ex-colony.

This trip was to be repeated many times over the next few months, until eventually they sent him to a teaching hospital in Toulouse, all of this was accomplished without knowing a word of French, never having learnt French until reaching the age of sixty. It had been my sixtieth uncelebrated birthday in that first week of our move to France.

For half of the time now he was off his head or rather aggressive, the latter improved with time as he understood what was happening and just lay on the bed. I often landed up sitting by the river at the bottom of the garden and crying, I was so unhappy and feeling so alone in France. The experience that I had on the days when he was unable to communicate with me, has helped my understanding, when seeing people coping with their parents or spouse with dementia, it's appallingly lonely when the person you love and loves you, suddenly doesn't recognise you and shouts aggressively at you, the sight of this situation fills me with compassion and understanding. Still at least knowing that he would be back again in a couple of days was a great relief.

The whole situation was compounded by being friendless in a country whose language I was unable to speak, but it really had its funny side sometimes though. One night in the emergency department of the hospital I needed to tell a neighbour that I had left my house door open. It was eleven in the evening so I asked the nurse for the use of a phone please and she told me I needed to get some etiquette's first? — labels — and what sounded, to my ears, like a fish — perhaps a babble fish as in the *Hitch-Hikers Guide To The Galaxy*. Well, I certainly needed one of these. It was the end and I burst into tears for the first time in public. The system had defeated me. It was identity stickers (etiquettes) and receipts (fiche) that was wanted. That was the start of the dreaded French system of papers and stickers for everything

As the years passed we managed to cope, the specialist in Toulouse thought that removing all medication would be the best thing, watching him like a hawk and as soon as he became a little odd dosing him with three litres of water and he was back to his normal self very quickly. Even so, he was in hospital at least for one week in every six, when it became overwhelming or too dangerous for me to manage. He lived for another five years — it was not all bad and we did get to Barcelona for his seventieth birthday.

We returned to the UK a number of times, each time there was a drama but we did bring the dog back. The comas got closer and closer until the end and we managed with the help of the wonderful French health system to achieve final care at home.

Two weeks before this event, we came home in an ambulance, as John was being moved into a separate room with a water bed. An extraordinary thing happened to me. Standing alone in our bedroom at that time I was putting my clothes into a tall chest of draws that had a mirror hanging above it, as I closed the top draw there was an amazing flash of light, immediately thinking that all the electrics had blown I looked up and saw my reflection in the mirror, the reflection of my head was surrounded by a massive scarlet and gold Byzantium type of halo, the light was blinding, at that moment I knew that the end was coming and all the help and strength that was needed would be there for the coming days, what was so odd about the whole thing was that I was not at all disconcerted by the display, in fact it all felt quite normal, I am never surprised when these things happen to me.

Chapter Twenty-One

> When you do things from your soul,
> you feel a river of joy within you
>
> RUMI

It was then in the final stages that I became fully aware of all the amazing love and care we receive — we just have to accept and return that love without questions.

The next two weeks were very hard as I was doing the majority of nursing around the clock and alone, nurses popped in and out helping me to wash him and change the liquid supplement bags, one or two of my new friends dropped by, but they were very few at that time due to my rather confined life, when he was encephalitic and uncontrollable, I cried to have to tie him to the bed with crepe bandages, it hurt me so much but if I hadn't he would have injured himself.

The children and grandchildren turned up for the last few days, he recovered a little and was able to recognise them for a day. It was a peaceful house his door was always open, the grandchildren swam in the pool that I had dug in the back garden, they popped in and out of his room to see if he was still alive, this way was good as they learnt that death was natural and not to be hidden away and feared.

By chance, I have been with quite a few dying people in my life. As if people wait for me to be there, either in road accidents or a shop, one person even changed her place to stand behind me and promptly died. They wait for me, then die, it's not a thing that I fear it's quite comfortable for me, a thing to be celebrated that someone has returned home to become complete again. We are the ones left behind or we think we are. They, that are passed, are so near and are so easy to communicate with; they are in another dimension and do not need the old bodies any more. Our passed ones are with us in a flash when we ask them to come. We have communicated many times since John's passing he is around me often and helps me with all major decisions; he also is with me when I'm troubled.

After he had passed, we met up and he told me that the reason for all the pain and discomfort he endured was because he wanted to experience the sensation of being totally dependent on another person. In other incarnations he was always in charge and the prime carer for all this is often the way with men, so it was for me as his soul-mate to step forward to take the role of his carer as there was nothing that I would not do for him.

So there we are, it was an agreement with him before we came this time. We have been together in many dimensions many times, and we will be with each other again when my work here is finished he will collect me, this has been told to me. One must be acutely aware that we must be very careful not to assume that everyone's destination in this world is what we judge to be good from our aspect. It's hard for people to understand that when in spirit we want to experience all aspects of life, fear, hunger, greed, lust, power, and loss, that is why we return time and time again. This is the dimension where we experience things more profoundly — it is a place of growth. We arrive in this place with a loss of memory — *tabla rasa* — and this makes the trip more effective, it is just a continuous cycle of experience that we choose and co-create for our soul's desired development.

This time around I have been in close company with many that have had shared — previous or concurrent — lives with me, normally I don't tell them, but when there is a sense of confusion by familiarity and if it won't upset them it's OK, I tell them. We return to learn much more rapidly than is possible in the other dimensions, here we can tie up loose ends to finish relationships that time ran out on and put wrongs right, help those that had helped us on other occasions. When there is a nagging doubt, an unreasonable dislike, or unfounded jealously, they are just echoes from the past relationship — with that person.

Those people, in our life, who appear to be so familiar from the start are usually old relationships and with some you might have had many relationships with the same person, many of my friends were sister's or mothers at another time, also some were brothers, sons, fathers, or partners, many were enemies in other times.

My sister Isabel is often incarnated with me and when she meets significant friends of mine she recognises them and is overjoyed to be with them yet again. In our home dimension we live in soul groups, but our human families might not reflect that, for instance my mother in this world came from a different but closely aligned soul group to me, she stayed on with me after passing to help me with my work. She was my guard and protector until I became old enough and wise enough to guard myself. A bit of guarding helps with me, as when looking back at my life I have passed through it with amazing naivety often being right next to certain danger that was invisible to me.

John was my soul-mate, we all have them but we rarely incarnate with them, he is a very old spirit and often incarnated as a teacher. On the other side we are always with one another, plus a younger man who came into this life for a short lesson to teach me to be my true self.

Never be embarrassed and hide who you really are and what you believe in. If people run a mile from you it's for the best. I do know that every person who parts from you makes space for another who will contribute to your life in a different or perhaps a more meaningful way.

Never hang on to a relationship, never fear standing alone, be true too your desires and that way you make spaces for a new opportunity or a new more fulfilling connection.

Chapter Twenty-Two

Let all you do be done with love.

Corinthians 16-14

THE changes in my life were becoming overwhelming. To start with for the first time in my life I am totally free to come and go with no obligations, freedom is wonderful it was a thing that I had never had, being brought up in a large family one always helps with the younger members, then my major relationship in life started at seventeen and my own family three weeks before my nineteenth birthday, plus I've worked ever since.

Never have I regretted my early marriage and family, but it leaves one with another whole aspect of life that you never experienced in your youth. I was now realising that the freedom, so envied in others, has its sad side many might never have found total love and trust in a relationship. When you live alone there is nobody there to miss you or to greet you, to your friends you are mostly out of sight and out of mind.

Marrying young and having one lifelong relationship, you also become used to being half of another, there was never a time to really develop as a person in your own right. It's rather like having a conjoined twin for fifty years. Living in close proximity to another you almost breath and think in unison, being a twin one must wonder what singleness is like, it's only when alone one has the experience of being able to develop ones own personality, and there is the time to think do I like this? Do I want that? Do I think that?

So here we go out into the world I went trusting and letting other people in allowing them to be close, having been so protected for so many years left me very ill-equipped for the outside reality, very soon having my fingers burnt and being shocked and feeling very exposed and fearful of being hurt, I was ill-equipped my trust was so naive, the inevitable happened and the hurts came thick and fast. It was at that time that I learnt to set the ego aside it's impossible to hurt me or you on the soul level, only ego's can get hurt, the ego belongs to this earthly realm it considers its self to be so important but gets in the way of true communication, it also takes umbrage, that is a wonderful word to describe it, its just a pain in the butt.

One of the first people to become a friend in France was found whilst attending a yoga lesson, at that time John was still alive. He had a guardian two mornings a week, one morning was for shopping and the other was for yoga. It was at yoga we met, she was standing in front of me in the tree pose, and she was dressed in a bright striped tea-shirt and red shorts. I asked if she would stand next to me rather than in front of me as it was making me wobble. From that day onward we were close friends, when she walked into my house for the first time and gave John a smacking kiss as if she knew him so well and saying how glad she was to meet him.

She has been with me in many incarnations as my sister, mother and close friend. There are wonderful days when she just kidnaps me and we go on a trip to the sea, as *Thelma and Louise* runaways. I love and need the sea so much, it is a place of deep healing. Strange as it is constantly moving and wet, but to me it is profoundly grounding. The two of us arranged to meet up at this time it's important for me, odd things just happen, when looking back it amazes me what I went through in such a few years, a decade.

My, now rapid, development is just zooming ahead under dizzying power, this has caused me many a problem. I had decided when in planning time to take on board everything at once, having no fears, there was nothing that I would not pile on together. If one thing worked why not try five things at the same time, this did me a lot of damage that has been repaired since and my progress is at a rather more sedate rate now.

My guides reported that there were, and still are sparks of energy flying from my head and hands, but that was the way that I had planned it to be before my coming here. All this has caused many a health crises and I was in dire need of my lovely caring new friend. I'm resigned to the fact that when wishing to use one of my own essences or crystals it must be left on the kitchen table in a small bottle for three days then put away in the cupboard downstairs, for me to hold or fill more than one bottle of my High Vibrational Essences at a time by myself is not good, as after rapidly becoming ungrounded and dizzy, I then land up on the floor and it's now become the same with the crystals.

It was explained to me via my channel a while back that I'm the vehicle through which things are made just the clear vessel. All there is to do is to be inspired to make them. Others will use and distribute them, my job is just to manifest them, and the only problem with being the manifestor is my extreme sensitivity. Every essence that I have made I have also experienced its clearing energy through my body, this is a lot of healing crisis to experience in a very short time. As for the rest, they inform me that they have the rest under control. OK, point taken I'm not needed to hold the world up. I just have to trust in *The Management,* learn patience and stoicism, as they informed me. Oh dear, patience rears her head yet again.

Some years after I had settled down and spread my wings socially, I decided that it was time to hold some simple herbal workshops. My guides told me different, they informed me that the time has arrived, for me get out of making the earth beautiful, and to step forward and take up my true role as a spiritual teacher.

Well, that stopped me dead in my tracks, as a more unlikely person for this role would be hard to find. For starters, I had great trouble reconciling my ideas with the conventional thought of Angels, Evil, and God sitting in judgement, in fact any conventional thoughts on Religion or Spirituality at all. I've always gone direct to source, human intermediaries are not necessary.

The time had come to have a serious conversation with my guides via clear channel, The first question was about the nature of dualistic thought as the basis for religion, The second was the fact that it's obvious that angels don't have wings, plus information concerning the origin of misconceived thoughts telling us that there was such a thing as a devil, and while we were at it what did they think of my theory's concerning quantum physics. Well, it was all very interesting to get their feed back, we are the ones to make everything so complex and mysterious, when it's not at all, and in fact it's all very simple.

No, angels don't have wings because wings belong to this world, they are mainly for birds. In the past it was thought so as the people were very ignorant then concerning energies, it was the only way to describe the visual effect, caused by ascended beings visiting this dimension. Those who are of a very high vibrational energy, when visiting, manifest in our dimension, surrounded by aura's of high energy that vibrates at such a high rate that it gives the appearance of white wings flapping. There is also no devil we invented him — notice that he is almost always male — this arose from the origins of the male/female contest for dominance, plus the influence of the early church instilling fear as a form of control.

Women held power for a long time because of the mystery of procreation. Amongst the first spiritual beliefs was the sacred goddesses culture. We then lived in a situation of greater harmony than now; more was achieved by cooperation than competition. Women were the central pillar of society because, by their natural function of childbearing and home-making, they soon realised that cooperation allowed for development and for the family to flourish. They had a very close relationship with nature and food gathering, and were also the guardians of the fire, that was transported with them on their constant nomadic journey. Early man was not brutish, it is only necessary to observe the animals and plants around us, all interact sensitively to each other and the environment. Why is it thought that humans would be different?

In time men realised that they had a part in procreation as well as women, with this knowledge they gained dominance, with dominance came competition, with others and the offensive stance taken instead of the defensive. The offensive stance on the whole is destructive and a waste of energy and resources, we can always gain an advantage by combining our efforts. Just imagine the brilliant and highly developed world we would live in now if we had combined all of our efforts, lived in harmony with nature as well as humanity.

Peace and prosperity has been achieved a few times in our history, when women held the ruling hand, just think of the empress Wu Zetian who ruled China from 655-705 BC. Unlike the male Emperors before her she shrank the army, encouraged agriculture and had a large court where all the world visited and traded peacefully with her and her nation As soon as she died, after a long and prosperous reign, a male emperor took power and defaced her writings and started wars. This is not a single case it is something that has happened repeatedly in history, in many countries it is almost as if the male has to take on an aggressive stance as part of the threat to his manhood, this behaviour appears to be fear based.

Over time for various reasons slowly the male energy began to dominate, as they desired others lush lands, they took them by force. This constant aggression moved the earth's energies towards the male, with the more forceful, combative, territorial and competitive stance. It is this aspect of the male energy that has now brought the world too it's knees it is so desperately out of balance.

The time is long overdue; we all need to help the world come back into balance. A small seed will not flourish in extremes it needs moderation, nurturing and protection. Before it is too late, we need the courageous males this world, to step forward and try very hard to be at balance between their male and female aspect — far too many are in the extremes of male energy— that is nothing but destructive.

The idea of the devil and evil came from various sources, there is no evil here other than of our making, and by fearing it we give it power. I often think that the devil portrayed with hooves and horns was from the early church trying to banish the ancient religious believes of nature worship. The god of nature Pan, with his music, joy, and sexuality, encouraged many an Arcadian frolic — that was what nature is all about, joy and procreation. The early church was not into music, sexuality or joy. The great god Pan, had horns and cloven hooves and it all looks like he is the scapegoat — very suspicious.

Since very early on in the world's development, women have consistently had a rough ride, they have continuously been written out of history even to the degree of defacing images of them. In situations worldwide where they held soul or joint power with the male, either ruling a country or in the early Christian church.

Historically, in Europe alone, the debatable figure bandied about was that nine million witches had been murdered the majority being female. In nearly all of these cases torture involved sexual torture — punishment for being female. There has always been a hatred of the power of women's sexuality — hidden, dark, mysterious — this is fear based, as all hatred is. In the majority of situations men have dominated women by physical fear and sex discrimination, and still do, in many parts of the world, and we know that it continues to this day.

One of the shameful consequences of wars that still go on now in the so called enlightened twenty-first century, and is not openly discussed, almost certainly because all sides are embarrassed and can't explain away such behaviour, is the savage mutilation and destruction of women's sexual parts. Not just a few women but in the last fifty years since the second world war many thousands of women have suffered rape, and mutilation, the number is phenomenal. In the continuous African wars this is often carried out by very young boys who are under the threat of death themselves, this is a form of dominance over the female, and used to crush and shame the opposing sides of the fighting male population, it is carried out in many parts of Africa — now to this day. The women often become outcasts and live together; they are not refugees, they are totally traumatised shunned by husbands and relatives who are too embarrassed to admit to such behaviour on behalf of men.

Mass rape still occurs in all wars, the systematic rape of women very young female and occasionally male children, the latter two being paedophilia. It has continually been carried out as a weapon of fear and shame to demoralise the enemy, this has been committed by both Europeans and Americans, as well as Africans in modern wars that have been and are being undertaken in our lifetime. The main casualties and deaths of war always were and still are women and children and old people. So why are the war memorials put up for the brave men who over ran-them whilst fighting for their imagined freedom? Perhaps, they might have just have preferred a life instead?

This same type of hypocritical behaviour continues all about us. In the so called civilised twenty-first century world, it is often in the accepted form of the shameful medieval mutilation of the human body that is the circumcision of both male babies and adolescent girls. These procedures are aided, abetted and carried out by both sexes. Everything that pertains to our human body has a purpose and is for us personally to decide whether to remove it or not, when we are adult, unless it is for medical reasons. It is outrageous that an adult can sexually mutilate a small child for their own beliefs, without the child holding the belief or giving permission. Our body and soul are the only things that we own and can have power over, it shows a total lack of respect for a child who trusts us not to abuse them, but to have there welfare in mind. Because something is a tradition, it does not mean that it is good. These last statements are judgemental I know, but it is often necessary to open the eyes of a world of sheep.

Always question tradition, every part of our body has a function, nothing is surplus or a bad design, especially any part to do with our sexuality, The religions of the world appear to try on all fronts to make sexuality a crime and by guilt trying to remove the pleasure, but keeping the procreation. The majority of religions are totally obsessed by sex and our sexual nature, it is through our sexual nature that the shadow side of the major religions have tried to exert control over us, remember that control has always been wielded by the use of fear, the threat of hell, and all the rest of that rubbish.

In this dimension you are only accountable to the source of all things and never a flawed human being working as an intermediary.

The feminine energy of the world has been put down for a very long time. Now that the pendulum is swinging back towards the female, it is time for this energy to rise yet again. Unlike what many think, this energy must come from both male and female, it is not from women alone. Let us hope for a balance in the near future with more of the cooperative nurturing feminine energy combining with the masculine assertive energy — keeping all things in balance and moderation. The pendulum must not go to the extremes any more, we are nothing but different sides of the same coin, both sides hold equal value, women no longer need to be pressured into extreme femininity nor males into extreme masculinity. Polarisation causes stalemate not progress, our soul is a balance between both sexual directions, when here we choose to show and use it in the direction that we wish to.

I hope all those who feel the call are readying themselves at this auspicious time for humanity to take a giant step forward into their true role in helping to change the world to come, each of us starting with our own small personal changes.

Chapter Twenty-Three

*When the door of happiness closes, another opens;
but often we look so long at the closed door we
do not see the one that has been opened for us.*

Alexander Graham Bell

THROUGH our many incarnations, we desire to experience all the many aspects of humanity and its emotions, the most base to the most elevated. It is only when in this dimension that we can experience the full range of emotions, this is the way to develop and evolve. So be careful how you condemn another, we have all been there. Never say that a human is behaving like an animal either as animals do not behave as badly as humans; we are all experiencing the many aspects of human behaviour, in all its extremes. My guides tell me that the human beings that display the most extreme of what we refer to as — *evil behaviour* — are in fact usually suffering from chemical imbalances of the brain and do need to be separated from society and cared for Remember that they wished to experience life this way.

There is no evil outside of us we just make it so by recognising it, recognising something empowers it. The light and love will always win, as it is both more abundant and powerful than the dark. We to have a light and dark side of all our characteristics, we take on Archetypes, it all depends on which side you chose to develop and give energy to this time around.

There are those of us here who wish to experience life with only the lower chakras fully functioning, in this way they can be cut off from their heart emotions — their interconnection with humanity that comes from the heart chakra upwards. These are the ones that we refer to as heartless, it is not for us to pass judgement on people, they are just experiencing life in a different way this time.

The side effect of being a manifestor is having to live with very *leaky* borders, these cause me to become totally entangled with all things when I give them my undivided attention. It is in this way that all the High Vibrational Essences that I now make are produced. One must suspend the ego and channel through to the energetic essence of whatever it is, animate, inanimate or thought, just become *at one* with the subject.

In time, I was introduced via recommendation to my clear channel. She came into my life when I was booking a session to open my Akashic records. I still do go into the Akashic records on all occasions, they are protective and enable me to communicate with only my highest guides so they are now opened by me each day when working and writing, or just being, they protect and guard me, so that I am open only to the highest spiritual information.

Opening The Akashic records was a wonderful "Oh yes, oh yes!" moment. At the time of the first opening of my records, I had been avidly reading everything that was available concerning quantum physics, and found that once the theory of this was applied to the spiritual understanding, all was revealed. It's all so simple our thoughts make it so complicated, we do have a habit of running round and round in our heads and not using our hearts at all times — the recognition of the heart is sounder, faster and more accurate than the head.

We are all here in many dimensions, repeating and repeating, no beginning, no ending, experiencing and developing, just being in fact. A human — being — not a human — doing — is the mode to be desired. In this dimension the energies are heavy, when we gain a physical body instead of our light body, we lose our memory of who we truly are, but this is the dimension where we can gain experience in all the aspects of human life, it is the place where we achieve spiritual growth at a faster rate. It would hamper us if we were totally aware of all our other live experiences, so our earthly brain is hopefully *tabula-rasa* on arrival, but not always, as many of us know, some things do come through.

My clear channel who helps me with my communication via the Akashic Records, told me that the time had come to be introduced to my senior guide. She said that he appeared to be a very powerful guide, and told her that the time had come for him to step forward and work with me more closely. I call him Grey as the name he gave for me to use is unpronounceable he said that names are not important as he has had many names over very many lifetimes, Grey was the name he suggested, so to me he is the beloved Grey, the term beloved is a sign of my respect for him and it also acknowledges the powerful bond of love between us.

He has a great sense of humour though, as when introduced he laughingly commented that he had strong boundaries, and needed them when with me. That, I suppose is because of my habit of charging about rather enthusiastically both physically and energetically treading on others toes on many levels and on many occasions — horses often don't know that when they are gazing at you lovingly they are also treading on your feet. Grey came to where he is now from the same training origins and lives as me, via the nature and healing route that I have walked through my many incarnations. My thread of evolving being from the place of earth and healing as an elemental, a wise woman, witch, shaman, and herbalist, call it whatever you like, it is in fact under whatever name, always a healer. Basically I still am, as these things never leave you, spending my time repairing and putting to right everything that crosses my path. It's an embarrassment to say but my life is as a doer and not one for having my head deep in the mystical clouds. There is definitely no mystic new age *wu wu* about me, born under the sign of Virgo with a Leo moon, that's a powerful direct fire that's both strong and physical.

Many times my incarnations are as a European, but in some others as North African, the rest are rather vague there is a strong sense of the Mediterranean as well as possibly Greece, Egypt? I never bothered to enquire, it's not important. I don't think there is a feeling of the Far East about me.

It's to no advantage to just idly enquire about one's past, this life and being in the now is the most important, always try to remain in the present there is no past and no future — just now.

It is wonderful to be working with Grey I am so very privileged and he in turn says he enjoys being with me. My channel sees him and told me that he is a very powerful guide, but so very caring. I have seen his face only once and he was eastern, a coppery colour, what he looks like is not important, it's just the energy. When Grey is nearby I am surrounded with blue sparking and flashing energy. The first time that I experienced this, Grey felt close, and the message was given to go to buy a stone, it was to be an aquamarine and through it I would be able to connect too him more easily as he will communicate via water, he said also that he would give me a sign when the right stone was found, also that it would not be where I expected it to be.

Off I went to the crystal shop to purchase a lump of raw aquamarine, though on receiving the original message I visualised it as liquid glossy and spiralling as water, searching the shop there was nothing that rang a bell, so disappointed and walking down the road I passed a jeweller that used crystals, I thought why not go in and ask if they had any aquamarine. The assistant showed me many hard facet cut stones at high prices, then at the end she mentioned that she had a ring with a smooth cut stone the price would be low as that type of cut was not fashionable. "OK! bring it out" was my rejoinder. As she showed me the stone without any warning the beloved Grey was there just behind my left shoulder surrounding me with swirling blue light and an overwhelming sense of his presence, with a feeling of such love that was indescribable, this love I was feeling was to overwhelm me many times in the future. Whenever one is with those from the higher vibrational dimensions there is an overwhelming sensation of love and joy.

The very first time I experienced this sensation was exactly one year after Johns death and before my car accident. I arrived back home from shopping, one day and remembered that it was the first anniversary and the time of John's passing. So I sat down and lit a candle on a low table, closed my eyes for a minute to orient myself, but not a second had passed before I was overtaken by an amazing sensation of being completely wrapped around with a sparkly pink cloud, rather like candy floss, and such comfort love and joy, then in a flash I was either on the back of, or was, a very large brown bird seeing the wings undulating each side and feeling the powerful movement.

The wingspan was vast and I was deafened by the sound of them beating as we flew, it was a terrifying experience. This was to be the first of my current experience's of flying.

We flew low over a landscape of complete devastation and ash grey, everything was destroyed there was very little life, the rivers were dried and cracked the land was covered with ash all was grey. Somehow I returned to the room and stood up with my body shaking from head to foot, even with my eyes wide open I was still in the middle of the deafening noise and movement it lasted for a long time at least fifteen minutes. The whole experience was a great and unexpected shock, starting with the feeling of being reassured and relaxed, and then made off with and the devastated landscape I wondered was it left over from the past, or was it to come? I was filled with foreboding regarding the future of this planet.

This experience was to repeat itself in dreams for quite a long while. I dreamt that I was always walking through empty city's flying low over dried out waterways just devastation, people walking with only the sight of their backs all of them covered with dust, when unable to take any more I slipped off to the side and walked a path of very green grass covered with yellow flowers. The next time when going through my channel in the Akashic records I asked my guides about my dream. It appeared that it had been a left over from another life when my planet had undergone great upheavals and had literally thrown me off in the great disruption. By the work I had undertaken with clearing and uncovering many submerged things that had surfaced my guides removed the recurring dream — thank goodness — and this memory has now been erased, in my dream's at night it is no longer there.

We often get leftovers from other lives a bit like a red sock in the white washing, many of our memories are very painful. Since that time there have been many flying trips — now normally and deliberately by my own desire. When flying or meditating it is very important to always stay grounded and bring the light and energy down, and not to go up to meet it. We are not here to ascend to the light we are here to bring the light down to this place and time, we come from the place of light.

The importance of being grounded is one of the primary reasons why shaman do their healing work on the ground; they are often depicted in illustrations in a squatting position, working on the earth. This is probably the reason why I find myself sitting on the ground to communicate with plants when making essences.

So the ring was bought with the intention of having it altered to fit my left ring finger, at that moment it only fitted onto the left small finger. Out of interest when returning home I went onto the Internet to check out what the small left finger represented. It was under the provenance of mercury so it was for communications, interesting, this rang a bell as I am ruled by mercury and have an enormous amount in my birth chart — so there we are, the ring of the juggler and heavenly messenger — it was intended to be on the small finger of the left hand.

Chapter Twenty-Four

> Your time is limited so don't waste it living someone else life. Don't be trapped by dogma which is living with the results of other people's thoughts, don't let the noise of other peoples opinions drown out your own inner voice, and most important have the courage to follow your own heart and intuition.
>
> Steve Jobs

THERE are many helpers from the other dimensions in my life now; they each come into our lives when we ask for help. The first to arrive in my head very clearly were Flo and Grace — go with the Flo and accept with Grace — they are what I call my back-room super women. Their job is to facilitate all things and to smooth the way, one only needs to ask for the solution for it to swiftly arrive and it will, but perhaps it will not be as one expected, they are truly amazing and this is a small tribute I wrote regarding them.

There is a clear picture of them in my head. Flo is tall and thin with a woolly cardigan a droopy bosom and a string of glass beads resting on it, her hair is greying and worn in a collapsing bun at her neck, Grace is shorter plump and younger she has a pink twin-set and a light lavender mix tweed skirt her hair is white blond and curly, both are of an indeterminate age somewhere between fifties and mid sixties. The wonderful ladies one would find in offices the ladies who knew how everything worked, they are my Superwomen. Since their arrival my guide told me that to show me what they looked like, they use one's own history and memories as a source.

Thanksgiving

Each day I say and feel thanksgiving

To my back room girls and angelic helpers,

For every task that is set for me

They are there, waiting to fill my desires

They anticipate my needs before I know I have them

They sweep the path before me, my thanks are boundless

My soul is having a wonderful time with me on this visit.

A few months later Arthur arrived, remember that I cannot see these helpers. I am claircognizant, clairsentient, clairaudient, but not very clairvoyant. I switched that off as a child, it was replaced by dreams of significant future events. I really don't like those much as it's often to disturbing, who wants to see disasters, it's all too much.

Arthur's arrival was very funny, he was suddenly next to me in the living room and was following me around the house colliding with me wherever I turned, he was very eager and excited to meet me he felt very kindly. I see him as of middle height and dark haired. I asked around my friends to see if they knew of him I was thinking of him as one of their attachments left behind, I was greeted by a blank no, so I asked my channel for advice. For instance, must this person be cleared — smoked out with sage, salt, sound, etc. She was silent a moment then burst out laughing saying that the comment had given great amusement to my guides as usual.

Arthur was a new guide sent to me to help with clairvoyance he is distantly related to me in my soul family and in his last incarnation he had been a fireman.

So there we are — another helper arrives. Often Arthur is around me and is very welcome in fact he arrives to help me in other ways as well. When I replaced my car, the first time I took it out on a very high and bendy road. I was getting rather stressed with the new gear set up, at the time I was rapidly approaching the bend at the site of my old accident. Arthur was suddenly at my side and stayed there, perhaps he had driven the fire engine? All was soon under control again and it made me realise that I can ask him to help with anything that he might know about, he always has a feeling of good humour about him. A recent contact with Arthur was surprising, about a year ago my guide told me to find a certain spring in the area as it would be good for me to sit by it to gain insight, search as I might it was to no avail it was tucked away somewhere for later.

In my way of communication via dreams I met Arthur in a dream as he wished to show himself to me. He was stocky with short crinkled dark shiny hair, glittery glasses and a very kind face, he came up to me holding a card with my name on it. He said that he was a taxi driver and had come to collect me to take me somewhere, this was all a bit mystifying as, no, I had not ordered a taxi, two ladies standing with me said, he looked OK, and I ought to go, so off I went with him. There was nothing more to remember on waking.

The next day having a particularly fraught early morning, in combination with being in a running away mood, wanting to go to the sea, off I went for my early walk into the countryside, this time when hearing a trickle of water instead of passing on by, I paused and felt compelled to grab a big stick and climb up the steep slope into the rocks searching for where the sound came from. It was no distance from my normal route, vertical, just above me; it was above me in a circle of rock that was overhung by a stunted oak, with an ominous amount of wild boar footprints around.

Sitting down on a rock I experienced a sensation that the back of my head opened this was followed by a feeling of great peace flowing in. I fell into a short deep sleep and knew that Arthur was with me, so thank you, Arthur for the help with finding my special place of peace. Next time looking up as well as down when walking would be a good idea.

When first starting to prepare the essences, there was a feeling of great excitement from a lot of the new helpers, and other's that were around it was extraordinary. I was actually being physically jostled in the crush to help and for them to see what was going on, the feeling is very strange its like being jostled by many excited giant rubbery soap bubbles battering me on all sides of my body.

The next helper to come along was Elsbeth, her name is pronounced with a lisp, she wears perfume and was a nurse and is here to help me to look after myself on a physical level as my life is a bit random. I often get very tired needing to be constantly reminded to lie on the floor and stop working. My vibrational level is fluctuating yet again at the moment as I ready to take on extra new things, there appears to be no limits to what they send me to do. This why Elsbeth is invaluable, but they all have my permission to remind me or tell me at any time of anything that I need to know or do.

Normally one's helpers will only approach in an emergency, unless asked. The latest one to appear in my life was Alistair, all that is known to me at the moment is that he is a precursor, as to what who knows? They don't tell me what things are turning up, as they say that would take the fun out of it, whoever these wonderful beings of light are they do enjoy a joke.

A short while ago while having a connection with someone who lived in the mountains, I was on a visit to their garden in early spring when I had an overwhelming urge to make a place essence.

The land was very beautiful; on one side of the garden was a torrent on the other side a raised wild terrace on which was a pool of snowdrops. I stood behind the snowdrops with my back to an ancient grey sandstone wall that was originally built long ago by the Cathars, this was the place for making the essence It was a place of such energy, looking across the snowdrops between two cherry tree trunks was a view of the torrent, when making the essence at the last minute on a fancy I placed a snowdrop in the essence as well, put the full amount of my intention into it, then took it home with me.

Some months later when unable to return I sat with the opened bottle on the table in front of me, immediately leaving my body very carefully I flew to the place where it had been made, my body was still standing there but it was hollow. Now slipping down inside myself and looking through the eyes at the scene before me I found that it was the same very early spring day, then carefully removing myself from the body and walking around the garden looking to see how everything was getting on it was by then a few months later in the season and the roses were flowering, panicking and thinking that I might be seen, I flew back home and carefully slipped back in to myself, I was still sitting in a chair in my living room, how long I was away who knows, that was my first really controlled trip out of my body.

The reason for being so ungrounded I was told via channel was because in a previous incarnation my life had been spent as an astral flyer working in a temple, for what reason was not explained.

It's not necessary to discover all about every life, for me only knowing of a few particularly those that had ends to be tied up or amends to be made for in this life, just knowing of my most significant lives that were lived in the area that I live in now, is important, there are many in my new life now who had lived with me then and they have come into my life again for a time of joint work and healing, we few brought light down then, and do so now as just a few can bring down the light of many when combined. Now is a time when many of us have returned to touch base together and put our shoulder's to the wheel of light for yet another effort.

Chapter Twenty-Five

In the practice of tolerance, one's enemy is the best teacher

The Dalai Lama

My other dimensional helpers have told me that we are in this dimension to manifest and develop ideas; they don't know exactly what because it is for us to be inspired and create these things.

We are creators of this world and we make our reality. The thought comes first, and when we do go in a positive direction we get all the help we need — when we remember to ask.

Often when new things of great significance to the world are invented things that give us a great leap forward, they come with the help of beings from other dimensions, they wish to give us a little nudge forward from time to time. They always have, they do it because of the wonderful potential of this planet, they so want to help us, we think we are at alone and at the pinnacle of human development but it's all just an illusion, we have a bit of an ego problem here our ego as well as our protector is our biggest enemy, humans think they are so powerful and the only ones that matter here, they often ignore their connection to source — that's just the ego not our true self.

In this world at this time there are many beings from many dimensions, and planets, remember, not all of us here are from this planet. Many are very old and due to pass on to the greater place of all energies and some are new; it is an ongoing cyclical process. I have a powerful feeling for Cassiopeia, and have never really felt truly at home here. Originally, we come here to experience it that's what it's all about, experiencing life in as many ways and places as possible.

A time will come when we realise, that all we need to do to develop is to make sure that we as individual beings are living our own live to its full capacity, and that means on all levels really trying to live with unconditional love forgiveness and understanding, resisting the human urge for judgement. Is that so difficult, outrageous or revolutionary? Try your hardest starting with the little things until it becomes the norm, given humanity's interconnectedness, this small step will eventually help turn the whole world onto the right track as each one of us is the whole world.

Just take your attention from the greater scene that is too big to contemplate or effect, first individually remembering to be loving, caring and forgiving towards yourself, that is not easy, it's always easier to help others rather than concentrate on oneself, but this is where we start. Because we are totally interconnected to all living creatures, only when we've cared for ourselves, is it the time to address ourselves to our neighbour and the world around us.

It's no good waiting for someone to tell us what to do as there is no big daddy or mummy, neither is there someone sitting on a cloud in a long white night gown, book in hand, listing your misdemeanours — each one of us is accountable to ourselves and we are the holders of the creative power, we all helped to create this world. We must each one of us stand up to be counted and live by our own truth, nobody will be punishing us. We just look to ourselves and constantly check out that we walk the talk, so be kind, understanding and caring for yourself first and then others. Don't judge the person just judge the action, fear is a judgement, love is not — in other words just take a deep breath and step back. We are so connected to each other and all things animate and the so called in-animate that are about us, there is no need for armaments or defences. If a tree were to represent humanity and the world, would one branch attack another? It would only result in affecting the whole tree. We are all just a part of the whole entity — the living world — so we are then all a part of each other, why would our hand be at war with our foot. We have been conned into wasting so many resources by seeing our friend as our enemy we do not need others as our enemy; we make a very good job out of doing that for ourselves.

Why should we put good development money in armament manufactures pockets, merely to kill ourselves? We have been filled with fear of our neighbour who is exactly the same as us, brainwashed for private profit and ease of control, remember people are more easily controlled when they are fearful of the common enemy without. It is a strange old and primitive idea of separate countries under separate flags, each a banner of aggression, when we consider it. We wave them about sing, some national songs and then the crowd is salivating desperate to sacrifice their young men at the behest of a few profiteering, warmongering, fools. I look at the world in general and fear that they are all in a hypnotic trance — we are reduced to fearful puppets.

We really do not need borders they are so outdated. The world has very few natural borders on the face of the earth and animals and birds move freely across them — it's just our primitive fear based behaviour patterns kicking in and being used for the wrong ends. Armies are completely outmoded as well, the very thought of putting the cream of our young people, the very fittest, the pinnacle of our development from the cave forward, into an army to fight and kill each other is bizarre. Its like some sick science fiction computer game for the simple-minded.

How any one person in any government in the world can say that they will press a nuclear button, is quite beyond my comprehension. They are unconnected to reality and must live in a fantasy world, the retaliation — MAD — mutually assured destruction — will be instant, wiping their country out at the same time, taking the whole of the world with them. If the man in the street said that, they would be locked away as a danger to the community. Those we put in charge of our future are completely deranged, they are the ones that walk through life unconnected to their greater selves. So do we invite them to be our leaders because they give the impression of strength, no strength and courage are different things, it is to stand up quietly and with compassion for the world and all its people, they are the truly strong ones. The others are hysterical bullies full of fear. I imagine that those from other dimensions stand back and watch us with incomprehension.

Why are we fighting still, has anybody come up with a sound reason other than spending a fortune on making the armaments manufactures rich? We can use the money, brains and energy spent on armaments to fight ignorance, poverty and appalling degradation that we as wonderful beings of light — that have so much potential — are constantly being cheated out of — it is both our birthright and the future of humanity.

Step into the future don't look back, the past will not create the future, the past has gone it can't be changed, just forgive and don't carry its baggage with you,

It's important to be in the present moment, as the future will come regardless so keep plans loose as there is only the now.

The time has come for change and you are responsible for it. Yes, you the one looking around for someone to "Do something about it".

Only when we all refuse to go out and vote will the governments realise that they are a complete and expensive waste of space, with their constant repeating pattern in all parties, and all countries, failures from the start of time, it must be faced squarely nothing is hardly ever done to change, they just shuffle the same amount of money and ideas about they, the political movers and shakers are nothing but jugglers — the puppets of the back-room powers of money.

They are an insult to our intelligence and a block to any meaningful future and progress for the world, they are voted in as our spokesmen and representatives, but once in power they lose all their energy and fire, they turn around on us forgetting that they are our servants they then become our masters, as in turn they too have become the servants of the powerful that are behind all things — the power of big money and influence.

We can create this change as individuals, from the inside; it just needs an effort to take responsibility for our individual lives and not pass it over to them the big *them*. Who are they? but pathetic humans working behind smoke and mirrors. There is no *them* and *us* it's just *us* we all have the same power to manifest the future to make the world as we would wish — we are in charge of our own small patch and that's our soul.

It's no good looking over our shoulders for somebody, the time is here for each of us to get out of the back seat, get up front and drive our own bus, we are not intended to be passengers in our lives. Do not go with the flow use the flow to speed your own purpose, only dead fish give up and drift into the flow.

One of the hardest things to achieve in life is learning to be true to yourself. We all get sidetracked with a fear of stepping out from the crowd and being alone.

Always ask these questions of yourself first. Where am I going? and only after that ask, who is coming with me? This is the opposite to what many of us end up doing, put it that way around and you will be true to your life's purpose, It's always hard not to be swayed by regret, guilt, or what I should do and what I must do, what I should have done etc. Now that's a word or two that needs removing from the English language, Should *and its companion* Must.

Just be happy treading your own true soul path, if a pilgrim comes level on the journey — they will — and if they prove to be going in the same direction great. Try not to deviate and search for one because in doing so you will forget your own true purpose, your route, and with that comes regret. Yet again, you will have cheated yourself out of your souls purpose.

Chapter Twenty-Six

*When life comes piling in on you,
just start sorting from the top left corner*

Angela Baker

So there we are. I was settling down to my new life alone in South West France, thinking that I knew what my plans were, a quiet life and just a bit of herbal empowerment teaching.

Then my guides stepped smartly in and explained that they wanted me to take up the mantle of making high vibrational essences, and I was to go forward with my metaphysical and spiritual teaching. They said that the time was now. I, having different ideas and thinking that I would stick to the herbal teaching, said "No, why me?" I was fearful to go there, it was not very comfortable doing so the last time around. I wanted this life to be safe and just wanting to carry on enjoying it, keeping my head down and doing just what was needed now, as I was retired. Life had been a rush with too much drama, the sun was shining now and I was resting in a safe place of recovery.

So there I was just doing what I thought would be a workshop on herbal medicine, when then by inspiration — again, was it mine?— doubtful given the cunning way they work. I decided to do the second lesson of the series on flower essences — choosing, using and making them.

It was long ago when training to be a herbalist that an opportunity came about for me to attend an extra course to learn flower essence making —my, now long dead, teacher had been very inspiring. At the first session that I attended she chose me as an example and asked me to come forward from the back of the group, immediately she had picked up on the fact that some months before my birth I was traumatised. The second world war had started and my arrival was not exactly desired or convenient, this trauma had caused an energetic hole in my heart, my teacher had picked this up from across the room, she was a very intuitive teacher, alas she died far to early.

One must always acknowledge the debt to one's teachers, mine have all been inspiring and still are, many have only ever had to trigger the spark to set me racing off in search of knowledge, and who knows from where that knowledge comes. Is it internal from our greater selves or from our own past memories, or external from this world? Perhaps from the Akashic field of quantum physics who knows, only our body tells us what rings true when we learn to be attentive to its response.

A few weeks ago I was reminded that the body's response was sound — not words or thoughts — it is immediate. If it's untrue we murmur, nah with a head shake, if it's true we murmur, aha, with a chin lift — in the future pay attention to your body and your first response.

The herbal lesson had a good turnout, the essence class was due so I proceeded to make an essence a few days before, just in case there was no sun on the day. Whilst making the essence I was strongly aware again of my long-standing relationship with the plants and realised that they had always communicated with me, life had got in the way, I had been too busy to listen too them a lot of the time.

Always when I passed one particular flower it persistently called out to me, it was my favourite a very ancient rose—Rosa Mutabilis. Wow! she was wonderful — so much to say, and so much to give. After making an essence from her, then trying it out on the class, they were using the essence in the normal way via mouth but they were reeling with the effect. It was only then that I realised they were being made in a different way, I was applying the practice of what I had only known in theory up until then, it is what is now referred too in quantum physics as *total connect-ability* —I was the plant. When making the rose essence I was the rose, we had no edges, we were totally entangled. There are days when I become totally connected to all things and people around me, all of this is sometimes very tiring to live with, I need to discipline and ground continuously, but being human I get over emotional and completely forget to ground myself.

I was unaware until when my guide informed me that I had a great knowledge of working with the elements. This is because that was what my training and working between lives had been about. It was also at this time that the realisation came that what others said was true, I am a very powerful manifestor and I must guard my thoughts. I was always thinking that it was the same for everyone, and that they all are able to communicate with everything, it certainly can be as we all have the inherent ability. Remove the bicycle training wheel of fear and believe — it's not scary. But I suppose that many just can't be arsed, they are totally blinkered, locked into life on the routine level and that feels safe.

Never let anyone tell you that a thing can't be done, as that puts a break on your power, find out for yourself, have total faith. Always know that what you are doing is going to work, there is no doubt in my mind that I have made essences in this way hundreds of times before, in other lives and other places.

When sitting with the plants and listening to what they wanted to give to us I came the realisation that in this dimension all things are animate, and that what we think of as inanimate is still aligned to our highest good and for our highest development. The whole world of plants and animals is here for us and we must respect them all equally, even the stones beneath our feet, they are but crystals in another form. All things contain the light of the power of the source, all things are the source, nothing is really inanimate — only the way we perceive it.

It was at the time of creating them that I made a decision concerning the essence, this decision was quite simple. I was never to put the home doctor manual type of list next to their description — listing a thousand negatives that they might help with, plus all the things that might be wrong with you

— this is not healthy thinking. Never read these things as words, manifest your reality and you will imagine that you are suffering from everything listed. I only write down what is relevant and helpful concerning the essences — what they will *positively* contribute to your life. It is also recommended that you never read the leaflets in the box before you choose the essence. Just douse the bottles or chose from the photographs and see which one keeps catching your eye or close your eyes and point. In fact anything you feel is the way for you, selecting one that way leaves the door open for both your higher self and your guides to help you.

When you read later what is chosen you will be amazed it's not the one that your mind — or ego — would have chosen, it's a better decision and rings all the bells. The one that you would have chosen would be from the ego driven part of your mind but the right one for you is from the soul. The soul is older much wiser and knows you better.

Recently when I was dousing an essence for someone who was extremely ungrounded — a method of divination that I use to determine a suitable essence — the douse indicated an essence that I assumed would be very bad for them. It was an essence for the upper crown, the douse continued insisting so I gave it, the effect was astonishing, instead of making them more ungrounded it had the opposite effect, a strong connection with their higher self was in order before they were able to ground.

A reluctance to incarnate is a very common situation, this is the primary reason that I do not use my brain or ego to choose, but just go intuitively or use a douse, let the soul sort out what is needed, its often a surprise. Stand back and let it participate in your life, communicate with your greater self and then see the difference.

It was around this time that I went ahead to make many more essence. My guides informed me that ten of them were very much in tune with the chakras and can be used for Reki and chakra clearing. My own view of the chakras is that there are twenty-two but my guides informed me that was rather in advance, as only a few thought like that, and it would not be in general knowledge for at lest fifty years, so I stick to ten for now.

These are the ten chakras. The feet chakra is represented by a brownish black swirling. The action is almost like a plughole. This clears the excess energy from the body, causing it to drain into the earth via twin spirals, exchanging in turn the grounding of negativity with the rising earth energy as it comes through to the body. The base chakra is red and at the base of the body. It connects us with our tribe family and roots. It is the home of the Kundalini energy. The sacral chakra is orange, deep in the base of the belly. It is the home of all creative energy and fertility.

The solar plexus chakra is yellow, it is positioned in the solar plexus, and it governs our self-esteem and sense of identity. The heart chakra is green, it is found in the heart area and is the body's governor balancing the lower more earthly chakra energies with the spiritual upper chakra energy. The upper heart chakra is pink, it is just above the hart chakra and is the home of unconditional love forgiveness and compassion. The throat chakra is pale blue, and is at the base of the throat, this enables us to always speak our truth with clarity. The brow chakra is indigo, it is at the brow the home of the third eye and the doorway to the soul. The upper crown chakra is white. This is the place where we merge with all things including our male and female energies.

Well, that was all a surprise to me as this information was channelled to me. That same set of chakra essences can still be used for many other things even if the chakras were their primary place of origin.

When thinking and working things out from a different angle, a thought serendipitously came in, involving the input of a gifted musician who has knowledge of the ancient system of musical notation. By being open to channel, and with a little time, the musical vibrations can be united with the vibration of the essence, they in turn will link into the crystals. Combine them all together and they will produce a complete harmonious system of healing, this will manifest in time, all things come at the right time for them to arrive.

Music was one of the earliest tools of healing, it resonates with the vibration of the chakras, clearing blockages and helping the body to ring true, the body's vibration should sound as clear as a crystal bell.

Close on the heels of the chakra essences came the second set of ten. These were to be known as the Soul Alignment set, they are to reunite us with our original earthly intention. The actions are revelatory, coming into effect swiftly and accurately; that is if people can resist the urge not to let the ego interfere with their doused choice.

After quite a bit of experiment and thinking I found the solution as to the best way these last essences were to be used. They were to be used in conjunction with a very special crystal — no, it was not me that found the crystals I was told, as usual, that the information was sent to me by my guides, that they really wanted me to use them, and they found it amusing that when at a meeting with my channel I had told her what an amazing coincidence it was finding these crystals, that they were just the right thing — remember, synchronicity is behind all things.

They were laughing as usual. I must be a constant source of amusement to those I call *The Management,* however clever I think finding something has been they have always had a hand in it, in fact they are involved in everything I do. There is free will always, but when the hint is dropped I'm off to investigate it.

A friend had given me a link to an obscure crystal supply, it was run by a man who was also a councillor for disturbed people. In his work with clients he used *self-healed* crystals, because the very action of the crystal breaking off and then healing itself made it suitable to go on to heal another. He called them counselling crystals.

> *I then go one step further and use three drops of the Soul Alignment essence on the crystal, that is then placed into an individual gauze bag that in turn is hung around the neck of whoever needs them, and for whatever the treatment is to be. Sleeping, Focussing, Commanding or Counselling. The crystals can be worn for between ten minutes and up to twelve hours a day. Their power is such that they only have to come within range of your etheric body.*

So, that was how I found a way to use such powerful essences, with the help of my guides constant tweaking and adjusting of everything made or done by me. This was all very satisfactory as the essences were of such a high vibration that they proved to be just too strong for many people to take internally. I am unable to handle them very often myself because of my extreme sensitivity to almost everything of that nature. When wishing to take one myself it's only necessary to place a bottle or a crystal with a few drops of the diluted essence on the back of the kitchen surface for a few days.

I have a good friend in the UK who works as a hands-on healer and astrologer. I took two boxes with me to give to her on my last visit. When she first handled her boxes she sat and talked with me for a while then suddenly looked down surprised to see that her hands and arms were scarlet, although not in any pain they looked exactly as if they had been scalded both the hands and up the wrist's and forearms were scarlet.

It was about this time I came to the conclusion that when using crystals for combining with essences or just to sit holding them, it would be a far better idea to have them raw — not to have them polished or pierced as this damages their vibration.

It is important also to be punctilious with the cleansing and recharging of the crystals, remembering to place them all on trays in the garden overnight when the moon is full. This includes any of my crystal jewellery as well, doing this simple thing will help to clear old negative energies from the crystals and will reinvigorate them for the another months work, helping to bring their potent healing energy into the house, for all who live in it and use the space.

As the chakra essences came along, they were swiftly followed by their respective crystals. These are not the usual chakra crystals that are chosen, they were the ones my guides suggested and when one goes deeply into the crystals meanings and how they are used, it is easy to see why they were chosen. It was around this time that the information came through about how to store the essences. It is necessary to provide them with a cupboard with doors and enough shelves to store all of them with space around each individual bottle.

The next information was to purchase a Herickmer diamond for every shelf, this is not as expensive as it sounds, they are very small and not true diamonds, just the name makes them sound like a luxury, the main reason for using the *diamonds* was to keep the essences at peak potency. When making space essences they need six months to mature before using and need to be kept separate from each other.

My guides and I know that these essences are made for all beings and will act beneficially for everyone including pregnant women, the autistic, the mentally disturbed, children, animals etc. They are safe as each individual will only take up what they need to be viable, they only have to be in the auric field.

Instinctively I do know that though many will use them, they will be of particular benefit to those living in city's, separated from reality and nature, those who have lost the essential thread that joins them with the very fundamentals of life the daily breathing in and breathing out of the planet, the essences will help people to reel in the line and join up again with their life's true intention.

Many are lost they have strayed from their primary path and they are desperately searching for the magic answer, the answer is not outside, it's within ourselves. All that is needed is a trigger, the high vibration of these essences will provide just that, they will cut through the spiritual as well as the physical confusion that surrounds all humanity at this time, they help to connect us, to the very quiet inner voice of knowing that is within all of us.

There are many of us in this dimension who have arrived here at this auspicious time, we are readying ourselves to take a giant step forward into our true role in making change for the good of the world to come. Each of us first starting with our own small personal change.

It is important to remember that your body knows what you know, belief makes reality so be careful what you believe. Remove negativity and remember constantly thinking of the future causes stress — fear. The physical body holds our emotions. It helps at all times to be in the now, as there is only the now. Don't miss it whilst looking for the future or dwelling on the past. Remember to be really alive in each day — enjoy the day.

All in all, this has rapidly turned into a rather busy year it was no coincidence that it was also the year of the horse and being born in the year of the horse I had no alternative but to be swept along and ride the flow of energy it brought.

Whilst working or writing in connection with the Akashic records I would ask questions that intrigued me as being kinaesthetic — feeling emotions through my body, and seeing pictures of thoughts plus colours of music and words etc. It was intriguing to know how my guides felt and expressed love. I asked them to show me how they felt love for me, the demonstration they gave me was a wonderful surprise, first to come is a feeling like a line being drawn down the left side of the neck from the ear to the shoulder, then a touch like a fingers pressing in the centre of each cheek until I smile. All of these feelings are visualised in thin black lines rather like 1950s furniture, that was all black wires and coloured knobs, the next bit is a line that is from the left shoulder to the right armpit crossing the chest in a slanting line then back to the left armpit. The whole is accompanied by an irrepressible urge to smile, they often run through it all when we first sit down to write together. I'm immediately surrounded by a warm cloud of their humour, it's rather like going into a room full of old friends with a running joke.

The way that I view their visual message or when I meditate is in scratchy black lines and dots, it mystified me, for a long time I thought that my Clairvoyance was a bit like an old film until I came across illustrations of the tracks of subatomic particles colliding. I now realise the illustrations were exactly the same as I see.

Chapter Twenty-Seven

You don't have a soul, you are a soul, you have a body

C.S.Lewis

WHEN working in the Akashic records one is safe and surrounded by friends, one is also reassured that all information is coming from one's highest source, and for the highest purpose. Being rather open and porous, each day five minutes before rising I have to remember protect myself from harm. I have a very good friend an acupuncturist who explained to me that the world out there is not always likely to be in our best interests, he taught me a small but significant routine to perform each day.

> On waking, visualise a cinema screen then place on it a young child version of yourself, you would never let that child go out alone with no protection. Then enter the picture from the right and take their hand and exit right, still holding their hand, say you will be safe with me today. It's a simple trick reminding you to care for and protect yourself, as one is always ready to jump to the defence of children but forgets oneself. I have been told and am aware that I have many protecting me on many levels, both in the ethereal world and the physical world. I feel their love and care very powerfully every day — not all angels are confined to heaven some are in our life as well.

It was my habit to wander about naively, completely trusting, with my unprotected light burning rather brightly, until one day there was a very nasty encounter from a past life enemy who wished and tried to destroy me, but who I in turn in the past, had harmed. So remember that not all people you meet from the past lives were your friends and you in turn might not have been theirs, we are humans and still in the process of perfecting.

My house is situated in is an area that has extremely harmonious and great spiritual energy. This energy lends its self to my teaching via small groups of seekers, I find a small group is the best way to teach people how easy it is to understand how we all can relate to the powerful skills of manifesting and commanding with the energies that we all have within us. Sadly most of us are completely unaware of this energy and without utilising these gifts life can be very difficult and unrewarding.

To manifest, it is important to work at conceiving the idea, visualise it with great detail — the more detail the better don't be sloppy. It can be anything that you want, a job, a companion, a home, an achievement. Really see, feel and smell it, see yourself doing whatever it is, see what you are wearing, how you are standing or who you are with. Only then throw that thought before you with a cord attached, its like making a bridge across a crevasse, visualise it before you then follow it. Everyday give it some energy, make a space for it to come in your life, it needs energy to grow, everything needs input. Absolutely know that the universe will provide an answer if you give it enough detailed information too work with. Never be feeble, know that it will appear at an auspicious time the right time; with enough intention a thought becomes reality, it does not just drop out of the sky, it needs working on every day. If you procrastinate, say you are too busy, you will not receive what you request as you don't really wish for it with enough fervour — passion is the power that moves mountains as well as people — so command it.

My guides have asked me, as well as many others, to teach and write. We are all being drafted in as it is of extreme importance at this time. We all have a duty to pass on our knowledge, it belongs to this world. So don't be a miser, knowledge like unconditional love can't be kept to oneself, send it out to increase as you can't take it with you.

I am now in my seventies and using my skills to teach and write. Teaching all the time would be far to an exhausting project to take on, as by the nature of my work I am inclined to be rather super sensitive to the energies of others. So my role here and now is to run small healing groups, write books and make the energies of the place here where I live with its plants and its stones. It is important to pass on the knowledge as nothing is yours alone.

As my guides tell me I am the means — the vessel to create their, as well as my desires here — and at this time. They enjoy watching the results of my creativity, it's a learning experience for us, everything is an inspired exploration of what can be done.

On this energetic plane we all use our store of experiences and abilities that were gathered along the way whilst on the journey through our many different incarnation's, nothing is ours alone so there is no place for private ownership, listen to the subliminal messages sent to you — those thoughts that we consider to be intuition. This is where inspiration comes from, it's simply creativity at work.

One such message to me was, — Time, Patience and Fortitude *— this is day one and some people are not ready for you yet, you must be gentle with people, it's often new to them. My energies are too powerful and always too impatient, it's important to be aware that as well as physically knocking people over I do it mentally as well, so its* T. P. F. *from now on.*

My home is situated in the South West of France, the Languedoc, or using the ancient name, Le Pays d'Oc. As well as being an area of great beauty, it is also a place of wonderful healing energy and history. It was not by chance that I landed up here it certainly was not a haphazard accident, even though we were on the way to Italy. It was John's last act of grace to get me here, we had probably arranged for this to be so when originally planning our lives together. By all accounts my most fulfilling incarnations were spent in and around this area as a Cathar as also were the lives of many of my friends. We all have turned up in what appears be to a random way — but isn't — and bumped into each other, again by chance — Oh, no! —plus we are all healers in our different ways, not at all surprising as that was a Cathar skill. It is important that we are here, we are all needed to bring our light together yet again — as the light of two when joined makes the light of seven.

On my arrival in France I was barely aware of the Cathars, although John had bought a book concerning them whilst in Africa, when he was in his twenties. It was a book that hadn't been read by me, as was the case with the herbal book he had bought me, and then when I got around to finally reading it I was all fired up to train as a herbalist.

Looking back at your life's track, traced into the sand, it becomes clear — everything makes sense and no detour was without its learning.

One day, I became re-alerted to the Cathars on an innocent trip I had made to the series of castles known as Lastours. John was having a good day so we went on the trip to look at the castles with some members of the family that were on a visit. Climbing up a track high up the rocky slopes, alone by that time as the other members of the party were in front of me, I was trailing along looking at the wonderful stones on the approach to the gateway, when going to pass through it as I became level with the hinge sockets. I was clearly given the message — You can't go through there — so I sat on the ground outside and thought what's this about. Upon returning home I looked for information on the castle and its history, it was written that on the final days of the siege the women in the fortress were sent down to the village and told they were not to come in. Obviously I had just picked it up from all those years before, nothing disappears. It's not important for me to go to any of the remains of the Cathars lives now, as they resonate too powerfully with me to be comfortable.

As a people the Cathars brought in the healing, light and education, improving the working conditions health and skills of the people around them, they were life enhancing and full of love. The Church crushed them with unbelievable violence, cruelty and intolerance. The behaviour of the Church shows all the traces of a fear divisive and hate based religion.

At the time of our passing we are not summoned for judgement, we just review our life with the help and love of our guides and friends. There is only unconditional love; this is the most important thing for us to learn here.

Never to dominate or influence another through fear as it is fear alone that is the true enemy, and a break on the route to humanities' enlightenment and return to the truth.

One of the best series of books to read about and understand the Cathars beliefs are written by Arthur Guirdham, an English medical doctor and eminent psychiatrist. He made it his life's work to interview a group of reincarnated Cathars that, without invitation, appeared at his practice over many years. He made meticulous records of their past everyday lives and beliefs, feeling that it was his calling and very necessary to uncover what their life was truly like. They were not at all as the inquisition records reported them to be — Don't forget who collated the records — At that time they were seen as an enemy of the church and most of the records had been destroyed. But with the help of a diligent French archivist much of the history has been uncovered that correlates with Arthur Guirdham's patients disclosures, recall also that there was no freedom of religious thought at that time. The church had immense power, this must never come about again, millions of lives are and have been lost because of intolerance.

So, as we see, fear and mass murder raises it head in many forms continually in our history as well as in the present time. The Cathars were a very wide spread community; much wider than people realise there were records of them flourishing in both Italy, the Rhineland and Croatia. The Cathars worked and trained others in healing with power enhanced herbal medicine skills, advancing education for all, teaching the crafts and skills to earn a living it was certainly not elitist, they also passed on the arts including music do not forget who the Troubadours were, musicians patronised by the Cathar community, and the reason why they travelled so extensively, their songs were not totally concerned with courtly love, it was groups of travelling musicians who passed on information and warning of danger from the church spies.

The Cathars were loving and life enhancing beings whose desire was to bring enlightenment down into a world full of darkness, superstition and fear, there was equality between the sexes and status in their religious hierarchy, their basic thinking though still came from a Dualist base. Remember how long ago the Cathars were here and how advanced they were, on many fronts far more advanced than we are now. Just imagine how the world would have progressed if such enlightenment had been allowed to develop. True enlightenment is a threat to the powers that be, they just dish out a feeble shadow of the real thing and humanity is duped yet again.

> *Never forget that we are giants of immense power in our real dimension, when here we use but just a fraction of our true abilities, we live in a constant state of forgetfulness.*

By all accounts living and working as a Cathar was my most fulfilling incarnation, even though my work with energetic medicine, was not so developed at that time. I no longer fear to step out of line and use my abilities in public view, it has taken me a long time and a lot of work to remove the residue of fear left from my earlier lives.

Hopefully we will all never forget the past and present pioneers that fought for all our freedoms on every front, not all of them were famous or in the public eye. Remember most were ridiculed at the time for what they did and believed — ridicule is another aspect of fear. We must be vigilant in this world to protect these freedoms from erosion or repression.

The area around the Languedoc was not just attractive to the Cathars, it was home to many other enlightened groups of people, both before and after them. The area contains a particularly large vortex, providing a very powerful energy, throughout the surroundings, many smaller vortexes are scattered across the surrounding area, a small one is very close by to where I live. This must have attracted me to the area and the building where I now live. Living in a place of many small energetic vortexes can cause local havoc, constant small slippage between dimensions, misplaced objects coming and going, the trick is to just ignore it, as all returns in time.

Being a very decisive person and having never dithered about anything or anybody in my life, and if ever that situation arose it would mean that I was trying to push myself in the wrong direction. When first setting eyes on the barn, even though it was a very unprepossessing derelict stone building, I had a knowing that this was it; but the sign on the front said it was sold, and it needed a lot of work and expense to turn into a house. Somewhere in my inner self I just knew that this was it, and I would settle here and make essences of a particularly high energetic vibration, even if my conscious earthly self was in ignorance at that time, and I thought that it had its own agenda and plans for the future. We all know what becomes of making plan's don't we.

Walk on the world lightly but with a powerful intention, when in this earthly dimension we are here to manifest the intention of source through our body.

Try to be kind to the world, it is at a pivotal moment in its creation, remember nothing stands still, so help by your every action to tip the balance a little in the right direction. It's never too late and every feather can affect the overall balance towards the positive.

It's no good trying to get anybody to change overnight but the easiest way to break a bad habit is to be conscious of loosing it over a twenty-one-day intention. Try to introduce one new thing into your life. That way, it will help to tip the balance. Nothing big, just a small thing for starters. This way, if at least half the population did so, it would make an overwhelming difference. I don't expect for one moment that they will but that thought should never stop you because you alone are a part of all the rest. So, take your power into your own hands. The time has come to step up to the mark and be counted. Not in a minute when you're not so busy but now as there is only ever now.

On leaving the clinic where I worked in the UK I jokingly said perhaps being in France will be about making flower essences. We often make jest of what turns out to be the truth, so it was with surprise many years later, the essences are being made of all those flowers, crystals and the very rocks standing in this sacred energetic place. Now I am making essence of the very place itself. Close your eyes make a choice of a bottle, open it then just sit with it; one then can be transported to the very place where it was made.

Recently a place essence was made on the site of an ancient Greek harbour in Spain, I was desperate to make it in the ruins, but was suddenly sidetracked. So, I left the road and crossed the scrub land to the cliff edge. Only after standing there and making the place essence was it visible, that I was standing in a circle of stones someone had previously laid out in the grass.

On my return home I chose a bottle blind from those that had been made in the area, opened it then sat with it. On closing my eyes I was transported to the harbour, the difference being that the bay now had three Phoenician boats at anchor. I instinctively knew what they were, although having no prior knowledge of what such boats looked like. It was only after researching did I find out that the Phoenician traded with the Greeks in that place and that was what their boats looked like.

It was spring time when the essence was made, at both the time of its making, and also when sitting with it later I was accompanied by Persephone the Greek goddess of spring growth, she came up from the underworld. What a delightful surprise, her presence must have been steeped in the surroundings of that ancient Greek port.

To make an essence of a place it is only necessary to be present, open and to become a channel, hold your bottle of whatever medium you choose and merge with the landscape and it's surroundings. I close my eyes, lose my boarders and just merge with whatever it is I desire to relate to, or rather what desires to relate to me.

One day I was remembering and found myself re-walking around an art exhibition we had been to recently and I was describing each painting and the sequence of the paintings as laid out in the gallery to John, my husband. Totally take in an occasion and you can revisit it re-live it at will, deja vue, profound events, places, suppers with friends, occasions of great love or joy, but also great drama. Be careful, it's best to leave some things well behind. Everything you have ever known done or experienced is still there nothing vanishes, when you want it again just reel it in and experience it, everything that ever was is still out there, there is no way that anything can vanish.

People arriving at my door nowadays have deeper problems and I in turn must pay attention to the removal of their energies from both my environment and myself. I am always keen to apply the rules of Feng Shui to my surroundings as it's of extreme importance to keep the energy flowing without impediment, through both the home and work areas. Stagnant energy in the environment and in the body has the same effect, causing blocks in the energy and where there are blocks around energy, there is discomfort and disease, making a place for negative thought and confusion to build and stagnate.

A head full of negative thoughts is no longer of use to you it is like a cupboard full of outgrown junk, it takes space and spills out. Examine everything that comes up, both physical and mental, say to yourself does this serve me well at this time or is it just an unquestioned leftover from a past thought that you have grown out of. Clear everything out that no longer serves to support you in the direction that you intend to go. We need to travel light if we intend to travel far and this does not always mean physically.

A cleared shelf is a space for something new that rings with true vibrancy for your life now, and the now is the only important time, everything else has either gone or may never arrive.

Some few years ago there was another of my very clear significant dreams this time it concerned shelves. A few years after Johns passing I dreamt that he was building a room for me, it was rather like a long greenhouse with a glass ceiling letting in lots of sunlight the walls had been lined with very thick plank shelves that had very strong supports. On stepping into the room to sweep the floor I was upset to see his back as he was leaving by another door. I then started lifting off my back a series of very large rucksacks containers, cases and boxes, unloading them and lifting them high onto the very strong shelves, that were already full of things from the past, it was not important for them to be sorted now later would do. They were not to be shoved into a dark corner under the stairs, they were to be stored in a safe place full of sunlight, they were my past life and lives they had value, but were not things that would be needed in my immediate future, whatever and whenever that was going to be.

LIFE IS ALL ABOUT EXPANDING AND DEVELOPING TO OUR FULL CAPACITY, REMEMBERING, THAT IT ALL COMES DOWN TO UNCONDITIONAL LOVE FOR ONE'S SELF AND OTHERS.

SO WITH LOVE AND JOY TRY BREATHING IN AND BREATHING OUT WITH A CIRCULAR MOTION. FIRST DRAW BACK, TO ENABLE YOU TO LEAP FORWARD.

THE NET OF FAITH WILL BE THERE

IT ALWAYS IS

FEAR IS THE ONLY THING THAT

MAKES IT INVISIBLE

FEAR IS OUR ONLY ENEMY

FACE IT OUT

FEAR BELONGS TO EGO

SO

TAKE A DEEP BREATH

AND

LEAP

www.ingramcontent.com/pod-product-compliance
Lightning Source LLC
Chambersburg PA
CBHW071732080526
44588CB00013B/2000